# PAIN  PURPOSE

A Guide to Healing From Narcissism

Cheryl Dyson-Bennett

Foreword by Gloria J. Oliver Carpenter, PhD

FROM PAIN TO PURPOSE

A guide to healing from narcissism

Cheryl Dyson-Bennett

FROM PAIN TO PURPOSE

© 2025 Cheryl Dyson-Bennett

All rights reserved. This book is printed in the United States of America. No part of this book may be used or reproduced in any form or by any means -electronic, mechanical, photocopy, recording, or otherwise - without written permission of the publisher, except in the case of brief quotations embodied in critical articles or reviews.

THE HOLY BIBLE, NEW INTERNATIONAL VERSION, NIV

Copyright© 1973, 1978, 1984, 2011, by Biblica, Inc. Used by permission. All rights reserved worldwide.
Scriptures taken from the New King James Version. Copyright© 1982 by Thomas Nelson. Used with permission. All rights reserved. Scripture quotations marked KJV are from the King James Version of the Bible.
Scripture quotations marked NLT are from the Holy Bible, New Living Translation, Copyright© 1996, 2004, 2007. Used by permission. All rights reserved.
Scripture quotations marked The Message are from The Message: The Bible in Contemporary English, Copyright© 1993, 1994, 1995, 2000, 2001, 2002. Used with permission. All rights reserved.

Designed for Greatness, LLC

Atlanta, Georgia

https://greatnesscoachingandconsulting.com/en-us/

ISBN: 979-8-9918242-3-1

Table of Contents

Dedication -- 6

Introduction --- 7

CHAPTER 1: All you need to know about Narcissism -------------------- 12

CHAPTER 2: Don't Bleed on Others ---------------------------------- 23

CHAPTER 3: Welcome to freedom ------------------------------------ 31

CHAPTER 4: Shining like a star ------------------------------------- 42

CHAPTER 5: Overcoming Narcissism holds ---------------------------- 55

CHAPTER 6: Life Jacket -- 71

CHAPTER 7: The Beauty of Your Scars — Turning Your Pain Into Gain -------- 81

Chapter 8: Owning Your Life--- 88

CHAPTER 9: Company of the Strong: Finding the Right Support Group ------- 94

CHAPTER 10: Memoir: Lessons from My Memory Lane------------------- 99

Conclusion: Moving Forward with Hope and Strength ------------------- 104

Questionnaire: Are You in a Relationship with a Narcissist?------------------ 108

Final Reflection: -- 119

Resource Page for Individuals Experiencing Narcissistic Abuse---------------- 120

Afterword --- 124

About the Author--- 125

Cheryl Dyson-Bennett's Publications ------------------------------------- 127

Dedication

To all those who have walked through the painful shadows of narcissism and are seeking the light of healing. May this book serve as a guide, a source of hope, and a reminder that no matter how deep the wound, God's grace is greater still.

This is for those who are ready to transform their pain into purpose, to reclaim their worth, and to rise with renewed strength and faith.

With love and compassion,
Cheryl

Introduction

Narcissism is an age-old problem in the world of humans. It didn't just start today, this personality disorder is almost as old as man, though, it wasn't until around the 8th century that it was given a name. The name originated from the Greek mythology, later retold by Ovid, the Roman poet. According to Ovid in his classic, metamorphoses:

Narcissus was fathered by a river god to a nymph called Liriope. Liriope once inquired from a seer about the future of her son, Narcissus. She was told that the young boy would live till an old age if he didn't recognize himself. This sounded strange to Liriope.

Narcissus turned into a very beautiful young man, highly admired by everyone. His beauty attracted many people who admired him, but Narcissus wasn't interested in anyone. His beauty was known by all regardless of gender. Echo was one of the people that was rejected by Narcissus, and she withdrew from the world to waste away. When it was heard by the goddess Nemesis, she cursed Narcissus and made him fall in love with his own reflection.

Being a hunter, Narcissus went hunting one day, when he was tired, he sat down beside a river and saw a reflection of himself. Narcissus fell so deeply in love with his image that he couldn't leave the river side. He drowned while staring at his own reflection.

The ancient story of Narcissus is not an irrelevant tale. It's actually very relevant to our society today, where many people are suffering from the terrible character flaws pointed out in this story. Narcissism, having its root in the Greek mythology, is a term used to describe a severe character issue where a person thinks highly of themselves and debase others. A narcissist lacks empathy for others but wants everyone to show concern for them. Their only concern is about themselves. The narcissist won't show affection to anyone, but they want everyone to sing their praises and be admired by all.

According to studies, there are several things that can cause narcissistic personality disorder (NPD). Even though the exact cause remains unknown, professionals believe that it's probably a mixture of some factors like early childhood experiences, genes, and psychological factors. The early childhood factor includes excessive praise or judgement by parents, abuse, or trauma.

Narcissism poses a significant challenge in society, often leading to the manipulation of others and fostering a toxic environment. It not only damages relationships with people but also brings numerous difficulties to the narcissist themselves.

The American Psychiatric Association's Diagnostic and Statistics Manual of Mental Disorders highlights these symptoms as primary when running a diagnosis of narcissistic personality disorder.

A person is typically identified as a narcissist if they exhibit at least five of the following characteristics:

1. **Exaggerated Sense of Self-Importance**: They have an inflated sense of their own worth and achievements, often viewing themselves as superior to others. This sense of self-importance is disproportionate to their actual accomplishments.

2. **Excessive Need for Admiration**: They constantly seek admiration and validation from others. This need for praise and acknowledgment is insatiable and central to their self-esteem.

3. **Preoccupation with Fantasies of Grandeur**: They are deeply absorbed in fantasies of unlimited success, power, beauty, or ideal love. These fantasies reflect their desire to feel extraordinary and unmatched.

4. **Expectation of Recognition as Superior**: They expect to be acknowledged as superior to others, even in the absence of concrete achievements or merits. They believe that their perceived greatness should be recognized by everyone.

5. **Belief in Their Own Uniqueness**: They view themselves as unique and superior to others. They believe that only other special or high-status individuals can truly understand or associate with them. This belief often leads them to form relationships exclusively with those they deem as equally exceptional.

6. **Entitlement to Special Treatment**: They expect preferential treatment and special favors from others. They believe that others should comply with their demands without question, seeing such compliance as their due right.

7. **Manipulative Behavior**: They use manipulation to achieve their goals. This involves exploiting or deceiving others to get what they want, often without regard for the impact on those being manipulated.

8. **Envy and Perception of Envy**: They frequently experience envy toward others and are convinced that others harbor the same feelings toward them. This perception reinforces their belief in their own superiority and exceptionalism.

9. **Lack of Empathy**: They demonstrate an inability or unwillingness to recognize or care about the needs, feelings, and perspectives of others. This lack of empathy affects their relationships and interactions, making them seem indifferent or uncaring.

These traits collectively characterize a narcissistic personality, reflecting a pervasive pattern of grandiosity, need for admiration, and lack of empathy. Understanding these features can help in recognizing and managing interactions with narcissistic individuals.

The Goal of This Book

The goal of this book is to offer a compassionate and empowering path for those recovering from the emotional, psychological, and spiritual damage caused by narcissistic abuse. Through the lens of faith, this book seeks to help individuals not only understand the complexities of narcissism but also to find healing and restoration in the truth of their God-given worth. By blending practical tools with biblical principles, this guide encourages readers to embrace their journey of healing with hope, to overcome feelings of shame and unworthiness, and to ultimately transform their pain into a renewed sense of purpose. It is a reminder that, with God's guidance, the wounds of the past do not determine our future, and that through His grace, restoration is not just possible—it is promised.

Why Did I Write This Book?

I wrote *From Pain to Purpose* because, after experiencing and witnessing the devastating effects of narcissistic abuse, I felt the call to offer a way out—a path toward healing and restoration grounded in faith. The emotional and psychological damage that comes from narcissistic relationships is profound, often leaving survivors feeling lost, broken, and unworthy. I know firsthand the depth of that pain and the sense of isolation that often accompanies it. I wanted to create a resource that sheds light on the destructive nature of narcissism. At the same time, I aimed to provide a spiritual framework for healing that acknowledges the pain while highlighting the transformative power of God's love and grace. Too often, survivors are left without hope, unsure of how to move forward. This book was written to remind them that they are never beyond God's healing reach.

As I walked through my own journey of recovery, I realized that healing from narcissistic abuse requires more than just psychological insight—it requires a deep spiritual renewal. It became clear to me that to fully break free from the lies and manipulation of narcissism, one must reconnect with their true identity in Christ. This book was birthed out of a desire to help others rediscover their worth, reclaim their power, and ultimately transform their pain into purpose. Through biblical principles, practical strategies, and personal stories of triumph, I hope to guide readers toward a future where they no longer define themselves by their past wounds but by the strength, resilience, and love they find in God.

CHAPTER 1

All you need to know about Narcissism

A narcissist is someone who has an exaggerated sense of their own importance, often to the detriment of their relationships with others. The term "narcissism" comes from the Greek myth of Narcissus, a beautiful young man who fell in love with his own reflection, unable to look away until he died.

While it's completely healthy to love yourself and have a positive self-image, the problem arises when that self-love turns into arrogance or a sense of superiority. This is what defines a narcissist: they think so highly of themselves that they view others as inferior or unworthy of their respect.

Narcissistic behavior has a profound impact on relationships. A narcissist often belittles their spouse, viewing them as less important or as a tool for personal validation. They may treat employees, colleagues, or anyone they see as beneath them with disdain or indifference. Family members, too, are often disregarded unless they serve the narcissist's needs. It's a deeply **heartbreaking** disorder that strains every relationship it touches.

Ultimately, narcissists struggle to form healthy connections because no one wants to be treated as a doormat or be constantly made to feel inferior. Healthy relationships are built on mutual respect, empathy, and understanding qualities that narcissists often lack, leaving their relationships hollow and disconnected.

Some Key Characteristics of a Narcissist Include:

1. Selfishness:

Narcissists exhibit an extreme form of selfishness, often disregarding the well-being or interests of others in favor of their own desires and needs. This trait is akin to the behavior seen in babies, who are naturally self-centered because they lack the mental development to understand that the world does not revolve solely around them. Infants cry when they want something, such as food, without considering that others have needs and priorities of their own. This behavior is perfectly normal for babies, who are still developing awareness of the world and its complexities.

However, when such behavior persists in adulthood, it becomes a serious personality disorder. Unlike babies, adults are expected to have a developed sense of empathy and awareness of others' needs. When an adult exhibits narcissistic behavior, it reflects a distorted sense of self-importance and entitlement.

A narcissist is driven by the delusion that everyone around them exists to serve their needs and desires. This belief is not always verbally expressed but is evident in their actions and attitudes. They prioritize their own gratification above all else and often manipulate situations to their advantage, showing little regard for the impact on others. This self-centered mindset is what differentiates narcissistic behavior from the natural selfishness seen in infants.

2. Sense of Entitlement:

An entitlement mentality which is a core narcissistic behavior refers to a sense of deservingness or being owed a favor especially when you have done nothing to deserve special treatment.

A Narcissist doesn't think it is necessary to do anything to deserve a favor, they feel you owe them anyway. A person with this personality doesn't think they need to do something worth honoring before they are shown a tremendous honor, they are convinced that everyone owes them that much.

Generally, life is built on a system of reciprocity; that is, the practice of exchanging things with others for mutual benefit. For instance, we say "respect is reciprocal", that is, if I respect you, you are supposed to do the same to me. And, if you respect me, I'm supposed to behave towards you in a respectable manner as well. It's a healthy system of exchange.

A narcissist doesn't believe nor operate with this kind of mindset. They feel everyone must, as a matter of obligation, show them honor even if they constantly dishonor them. A narcissist thinks even if they disrespect you in a terrible way, it is forbidden for you to dishonor them.

3. Total Lack of Empathy:

Empathy is the ability to understand other people's feelings and needs. Empathy takes a lot of selflessness because it requires one to put themselves in other people's position to feel what they feel or how they feel about certain things.

The fact that empathy requires selflessness makes it difficult for a narcissist to practice. A narcissist is an extremely self-centered person who has no form of concern about other people's feelings or needs.

The irony of this, which is also what makes it absurd, is that, even though a narcissist doesn't care or show concern about how others feel or other's needs, they expect others to be greatly concerned about their needs and feelings.

4. Overblown Need for Admiration:

Narcissists actually deal with internal insecurity covered up with a lot of arrogance.

Narcissists turn to admiration from others to feel great about themselves and cover up their own inadequacies which are usually obvious to them. Narcissists "eat" praise and admiration like food; it keeps them going. This explains the reason they tie down anyone they are using as an object to sing their praises and admiration to feel great about themselves. They trample on such individuals. Because a narcissist doesn't really have a good self-image about themself, they rely on excessive admiration and praise from others to feel good about themselves.

Five Types of People Narcissists Target as their Victims

Narcissists are often highly strategic in their interactions. They are skilled at identifying individuals who, consciously or unconsciously, make ideal targets for their manipulation and control. According to psychologists and human behavior experts, narcissists are drawn to specific personality traits or vulnerabilities that make certain people more susceptible to their tactics.

Here are five types of individuals that narcissists often target as victims:

1. Vulnerable People

Narcissists are often unconsciously attracted to individuals who mirror their own insecurities or vulnerabilities. Vulnerable narcissists, for example, are highly sensitive to criticism or rejection, and they typically seek out people who share similar emotional wounds. These individuals might struggle with low self-esteem, anxiety, or unresolved personal issues that make them more likely to tolerate unhealthy behavior.

The narcissist's ability to **exploit emotional vulnerability** makes them particularly dangerous for people who are struggling with insecurity, self-doubt, or past trauma. The narcissist will prey on their need for validation, providing just enough affection or attention to hook them in, all the while reinforcing their insecurities. This creates a cycle of dependence, where the victim becomes emotionally entangled with someone who constantly chips away at their self-worth.

2. Accomplished People

While narcissists often thrive on admiration and validation, **flamboyant narcissists**—those with an exaggerated sense of self-worth—are particularly drawn to individuals who can **elevate their image** or provide them with the status they crave. They tend to gravitate toward people who are **successful,** accomplished, or highly regarded in their fields. These narcissists seek out high-achieving individuals because associating with them boosts their own sense of importance and feeds their inflated ego.

This type of narcissist is condescending and dismissive toward people they perceive as beneath them, and they will go to great lengths to align themselves with those who can **help them maintain a façade of superiority**. In relationships with accomplished individuals, narcissists will often flatter, mimic, or attach themselves to the successful person to gain access to their social circles, resources, or opportunities.

3. Empaths

Narcissists are instinctively drawn to **empaths**—people who have a deep capacity for understanding and compassion. Empaths are naturally giving and caring, often willing to go out of their way to nurture and support others. They are incredibly attuned to the emotions of those around them and often find themselves trying to help or heal the people they care about. Narcissists see empaths as **endless sources of emotional supply**.

However, the relationship is always unbalanced. While an empath will pour their compassion and energy into trying to understand and accommodate the narcissist, the narcissist will never reciprocate that empathy. Instead, they exploit the empath's nurturing nature for their own gain. Narcissists have little to no empathy for others, and **they will manipulate empaths** by demanding more and more of their emotional energy, leaving the empath feeling drained, misunderstood, and emotionally depleted.

4. People with Unhealed Trauma

Individuals who have experienced **unhealed trauma**—whether it be from childhood, previous relationships, or other painful experiences—are particularly vulnerable to narcissistic abuse. Trauma survivors often carry deep emotional wounds that affect their self-esteem, making them more likely to tolerate mistreatment or even seek out relationships that are familiar, even if those relationships are harmful.

Narcissists target these individuals because they **can be easily controlled**. Traumatized individuals may feel unworthy of love or care, which makes them more susceptible to the narcissist's manipulation. Narcissists take advantage of their **low self-worth** and use it to their advantage, gaslighting their victims and making them believe they are undeserving of better treatment. As a result, people with unhealed trauma may remain in toxic relationships, constantly trying to "fix" or "save" the narcissist, even as their own emotional well-being is eroded.

5. Highly Responsible People

Some of the most virtuous individuals—those with a **strong sense of responsibility**—are often the ones most susceptible to narcissistic abuse. These are the people who take accountability for their actions, never shy away from fulfilling their duties, and believe that **everyone has a responsibility to contribute to the greater good**. Because they are so driven by their sense of duty, they often put others' needs ahead of their own.

Narcissists are experts at **shifting blame**, and they will quickly identify highly responsible individuals who will take on the **burden of the narcissist's mistakes**. A narcissist will place the blame for their actions on the victim, knowing that these individuals will absorb the responsibility, often out of guilt or a strong desire to maintain harmony. The narcissist will continue to push the victim to extremes, making them feel **personally responsible for the narcissist's emotional state** or the consequences of their behavior.

Ultimately, this dynamic leads to **burnout and emotional exhaustion** for the highly responsible person. Narcissists are never satisfied with how much responsibility is taken, and they will continue to demand more, wearing down their victims until they are emotionally drained and physically exhausted.

The types of people narcissists target are not random. Narcissists are highly adept at identifying **vulnerabilities** that they can exploit for their own gain. They are drawn to those who have emotional needs, low self-esteem, a strong desire to help others, or a sense of responsibility they can manipulate.

If you recognize yourself in any of these descriptions, it's important to understand that **you are not to blame** for being targeted. Narcissists are skilled manipulators, and they will take advantage of anyone they see as an easy source of emotional supply. Healing from narcissistic abuse involves recognizing these patterns, setting firm boundaries, and working on building a stronger sense of self-worth. You deserve respect, compassion, and healthy relationships—not manipulation or exploitation.

How Narcissists Bait their Victims

Baiting is a tactic used by narcissists to provoke an emotional reaction from their victims, often as a means of control. It's a manipulative strategy that narcissists employ to trigger a specific response, knowing that their actions will stir up feelings of anger, frustration, confusion, or anxiety in the other person. The purpose is never about resolving conflict or addressing an issue; instead, it's about **eliciting a reaction** that reinforces the narcissist's sense of power and control.

Narcissists thrive on **manipulation**, and baiting is a key part of their arsenal. They deliberately push their victims' emotional buttons, often in subtle or passive-aggressive ways, to elicit the reaction they desire. Whether through insults, guilt-trips, contradictions, or inflammatory comments, their goal is to create a scenario in which their victim feels triggered and responds emotionally.

The narcissist **delights in the reaction** because it affirms their ability to control and dominate the situation. When they provoke an emotional outburst, the narcissist feels a surge of superiority—**they feel in control**. The victim's reaction becomes a source of **narcissistic supply**, feeding their ego and reinforcing their belief in their own power and importance.

For the narcissist, **emotional reactions from others** serve as a form of validation. They know that their manipulative behavior can spark a response, and that power dynamic is what they crave. Whether the victim gets angry, upset, or defensive, the narcissist uses these emotions to maintain control over the interaction, leaving the victim feeling emotionally drained and often questioning their own reactions.

This process is not only about manipulation but also about **emotional regulation** for the narcissist. They use the reactions they provoke to **self-soothe**—to reinforce their sense of control and superiority, and to distract themselves from their own inner emptiness or insecurity. The more they can control the emotions of others, the less they must confront their own emotional vulnerabilities.

Some of the Baiting Tactics used by Narcissists

1. Stirring up Fear and Panic

When people are afraid, they rarely act rationally. **Fear** has the power to override logic and reason, causing emotions to take control of decision-making and behavior. Narcissists are keenly aware of this human vulnerability, and they often use fear as a tool to manipulate and control their victims.

A narcissist who wants to **manipulate through fear** will seek out whatever triggers the victim's anxiety, insecurity, or sense of powerlessness. By exploiting these fears, the narcissist can ensure that the victim responds in a way that benefits them—often by provoking compliance, submission, or silence.

Take, for example, the story of a young man working under a **narcissistic boss**. He had recently graduated with poor grades, and his self-esteem was low. His timidity and fear of failure made him feel **lucky** just to have secured a job. The narcissistic boss recognized this and used it to manipulate him without remorse.

The young man was being underpaid for the work he was doing. His boss regularly assigned him tasks outside of his job description, and on top of that, he was verbally abusive, insulting and belittling him at every turn. The young man was afraid to speak up because he feared he would lose the job, and with his lack of experience and qualifications, he believed he wouldn't be able to find another opportunity.

Whenever the employee began to muster the courage to confront his boss or assert himself, the narcissist would **threaten to fire him**, saying things like, "Who on earth would hire someone as useless as you? I'm doing you a favor by letting you stay here. Only I can tolerate your incompetence." These words would **shatter whatever confidence** the young man had left, reinforcing his belief that he was undeserving of respect and that no one else would ever hire him.

Over time, the employee's **self-worth** was completely drained. He was left feeling exhausted, emotionally beaten down, and utterly powerless—until one day, he found the courage to **call the boss's bluff**. He stood up to the narcissistic boss in a moment of unexpected bravery, refusing to be intimidated any longer.

The boss, who had always thought he held all the power, was **shocked**. He believed he had the young man cornered, that he had complete control over him, but this moment of defiance shattered that illusion. The boss had underestimated the employee's resilience—the part of the human spirit that refuses to be **dominated forever**, no matter how deeply the manipulation runs.

There is something inherent in human nature—a **desire for freedom and dignity**—that cannot be fully suppressed by fear, no matter how powerful the manipulation. Even in the most oppressive situations, there's something inside us that rebels against **subjugation**. This, I believe, is part of the divine design. Humans were designed to exercise authority, not to live in subjugation.

Narcissism is a direct contradiction to this fundamental part of our nature. It seeks to enslave the spirit and manipulate the very essence of what it means to be human. Narcissists prey on our vulnerabilities, but the drive for **self-respect** and **freedom** is stronger than they realize. This is why narcissism is not just harmful to individuals—it is ultimately a threat to the fabric of **human society**, undermining the very principles of equality and mutual respect that are necessary for a healthy and thriving community.

2. False Accusations

One of the most insidious tactics narcissists use to bait their victims is making **false accusations**. They fabricate events or distort reality to provoke an emotional reaction, often when they feel they're losing control or no longer have the upper hand. This is a common manipulative strategy, designed not only to **distract** you from their own wrongdoings but also to shift the blame onto you.

False accusations are a way for narcissists to create chaos and regain control of a situation. They know that by accusing you of something outrageous, they can **disrupt your emotional state**, confuse you, and force you into a defensive position. The accusation doesn't even have to be believable—it's the emotional chaos and **disruption** that they seek.

For example, consider the story of a **narcissistic husband** who tried to control his wife by cutting off the monthly allowance he had been giving her. He stopped the payments and watched to see how she would react. The wife, however, was aware of his manipulation tactics and decided not to give him the satisfaction of seeing her emotional response. Instead, she decided to tighten her personal budget, reducing her expenses to avoid any confrontation.

After several months of this quiet resistance, the husband couldn't stand it anymore. His need for **control** and **attention** outweighed his patience. He decided to launch a **dramatic and baseless accusation**, claiming that his wife was unfaithful. He fabricated a story about witnesses seeing her with various men in hotels, suggesting that her ability to manage her personal expenses—despite his withholding of her allowance—was proof of her infidelity.

This scenario is a textbook example of narcissistic behavior. Narcissists become **unhinged** when they lose control, or when they feel they no longer have your full attention. When that happens, they resort to extreme measures to destabilize you and regain their dominance. They obsessively try to figure out your every move—not because they care, but to **gather ammunition** they can later use to attack, manipulate, and reassert control.

In this case, the husband's false accusations were not just an attack on his wife's character, but a deliberate strategy to destabilize her, emotionally and mentally. By accusing her of infidelity, he sought to **undermine her credibility**, provoke guilt or shame, and deflect attention away from his own **controlling behavior**. It wasn't about the truth—it was about **keeping the focus on him** and keeping her emotionally off-balance.

Narcissists are experts at creating confusion. They craft stories that make you doubt your own reality, knowing that emotional turmoil will keep you **engaged** with them. The end goal is always to maintain control, deflect attention from their own flaws, and keep you emotionally **dependent** on them. Their manipulations are designed to reinforce their sense of superiority and keep you in a perpetual state of uncertainty, ensuring that they remain at the center of your world.

CHAPTER 2
Don't Bleed on Others

Narcissism is characterized by an **inflated sense of self-importance** and a **lack of empathy** for the feelings and needs of others. People with narcissistic traits often have a deep disregard for how their actions affect those around them. According to research, narcissistic behaviors typically have their roots in childhood experiences. A child who receives **excessive praise** or, conversely, is subjected to **harsh criticism** may develop an unrealistic sense of their own value or an overcompensation for deep-seated insecurities.

In some cases, narcissism can stem from **childhood trauma** or **neglect**, leading to a **low self-image**. To cope with these feelings, the individual may become preoccupied with asserting their superiority over others or seeking **constant validation** to mask their vulnerabilities.

The most dangerous aspect of narcissism, however, is the **devastating impact it has on its victims**. Research shows that individuals who experience narcissistic abuse may, over time, develop **narcissistic tendencies themselves**. This phenomenon is often referred to as the **cycle of abuse**—a situation where someone who was abused in childhood or in a relationship becomes an abuser themselves. The victim, instead of healing from the trauma, internalizes the toxic behaviors they experienced, adopting those same abusive patterns in their own relationships.

This cycle is particularly prevalent among those who have endured narcissistic abuse. Without the proper intervention or support, they may unknowingly **replicate** the abusive behaviors of their narcissistic abuser, causing a tragic perpetuation of harm. Instead of addressing their pain and seeking the necessary help, they begin to mirror the **manipulation, control,** and **disregard for others' feelings** that they once suffered.

Breaking the cycle of narcissistic abuse requires a conscious effort to heal, understand the dynamics of abuse, and receive support through therapy or other means of self-care. If not addressed, however, the pattern can continue, leaving deep emotional scars on all involved.

In Love with a Narcissist

Loving a narcissist can feel like an emotional trap. A narcissist fundamentally believes that **everyone owes them love, admiration, and respect**, while they owe no one anything—especially not affection or empathy. How do you love someone who holds the firm conviction that you must love and respect them, yet they feel entitled to treat you however they please? It is emotionally draining and incredibly frustrating.

This was the reality for **Kate**.

Kate, a beautiful and financially independent woman in her mid-30s, had always hoped to find a man who would love and cherish her. She was in a season of life where she was **open** to love, yet the pressure was building. Most of her friends were married, some with children, and every time she saw them, the disparity between their happiness and her own sense of loneliness became more evident. Kate felt the weight of her **singlehood** more than ever before, despite being surrounded by good, supportive friends.

One day, on a vacation, Kate met **Jim**, a successful and charismatic man in his late 30s. Jim was tall, handsome, and effortlessly stylish—everything Kate had ever dreamed of in a partner. Their chemistry was undeniable, and before long, they were in a relationship. Kate felt like she had finally found her **knight in shining armor**—the man who would end her years of singleness and loneliness. Her friends were thrilled for her, teasing her not to neglect them for her new boyfriend.

But after four months together, Kate began noticing disturbing behavior. At first, she chalked it up to minor quirks, but as the same patterns repeated themselves, she realized she was dealing with a **narcissist**.

Jim's sense of **self-importance** was overwhelming. He acted as though he was doing Kate a favor simply by being in the relationship. His words to her were more like **commands** that she was expected to follow, while her own opinions or feelings didn't matter. He had no empathy for her concerns, brushing them off as unimportant.

Within a few months, Kate had drastically reduced her interactions with her close friends. At first, they thought it was just the typical **honeymoon phase**, but soon they realized that Jim was the one who had instructed her to distance herself. **Isolation** is a key strategy for narcissists: they don't want to show affection, nor do they want their victims to get attention from anyone else. Narcissistic abuse thrives in **isolation**, where the victim is cut off from those who care about them and who might help them see the truth.

Kate was in shock. The man she had fallen for—the charming, confident man she had met months ago—had transformed into someone completely different. **Consumed by his sense of superiority and entitlement**, Jim seemed like a stranger. Kate felt like her world was **crumbling**. Jim had become everything to her, and at first, the idea of leaving him seemed unimaginable. The thought of starting over, finding someone new, terrified her.

However, Kate's friends rallied around her, providing the support and encouragement she needed to leave the toxic relationship. The importance of a **support system** for victims of narcissistic abuse cannot be overstated. With their help, Kate eventually found the courage to end the relationship.

Two years later, Kate married another man—someone who treated her with the kindness and respect she deserved. It was during this time that she met a woman who knew Jim from childhood. This woman revealed something that shocked Kate: **Jim hadn't always been like this**. His narcissistic tendencies had developed after years of **abuse** at the hands of his father, and the trauma from his childhood had shaped him into the man he had become.

The woman explained that Jim's father was a full-blown narcissist—arrogant, controlling, and emotionally abusive. He treated everyone around him with

contempt, including his wife and young son, Jim. Though he was a successful businessman who provided for his family financially, he demanded to be **worshiped** in return. His wife was stripped of any autonomy and was treated no differently than a servant in their home. Over time, Jim internalized his father's **toxic behaviors**, and these attitudes became part of his identity.

This story is a stark reminder that many narcissistic tendencies trace back to **childhood**. Children are in their formative years and, without proper guidance, often **internalize** both positive and negative behaviors from their environment. When raised by a narcissistic or abusive parent, children are more likely to develop similar behaviors as they grow. They **mirror** what they see, and if they don't receive the help or intervention they need, these patterns can continue into adulthood.

Don't Bleed on Others

One of the most tragic outcomes of narcissistic abuse is that many victims, without the necessary healing or support, end up repeating the cycle of abuse. In the absence of intervention, victims can unknowingly internalize the behaviors of their abusers, ultimately becoming abusers themselves. Narcissistic abuse can leave deep emotional scars that, if left unaddressed, can distort a person's view of themselves and others. Here are two keyways to how this happens:

1. Internalizing the Behavior of the Abuser

Numerous studies have shown the prevalence of the **circle of abuse**, where victims of narcissistic abuse eventually adopt the same toxic behaviors they suffered. This process often begins subconsciously, especially in childhood, when children internalize the abusive behaviors they witness or endure. They may not even realize they are absorbing these harmful traits. Over time, these internalized behaviors manifest in their own actions, sometimes without them recognizing it.

In adulthood, the effects can be just as damaging. Victims of narcissistic abuse may have their sense of self-worth shattered, and without proper intervention, they may start mimicking the abusive attitudes and manipulative behaviors of their abusers. Some victims even go on to inflict the same emotional harm on others that was done to them, perpetuating the cycle of narcissistic abuse. This **vicious cycle** is often referred to as a "demonic circle," where the emotional damage from one person spreads to others, creating a continuous loop of pain.

2. Transference of Aggression

Another common outcome of narcissistic abuse is **transferring aggression**—where the pain and frustration from past abuse are projected onto innocent people who were not responsible for the hurt. Victims may find themselves reacting to situations or individuals based on past trauma, not because the present circumstances warrant it, but because they haven't processed the anger and pain they experienced.

For example, a woman who was in a toxic relationship with a narcissistic man for years finally meets someone new. This new person, who happens to share the same name as her abusive ex, is a **kind, caring, and respectful** man. However, because of the emotional scars left by her previous relationship, she **rejects** him entirely, associating him with the abuse she endured. It may seem illogical, but it's a common response—victims of narcissistic abuse sometimes find it impossible to separate one person from another, even if they have no reason to.

I've heard of cases where someone was betrayed by a partner of the opposite sex and, as a result, they began **stereotyping** and distrusting everyone of that gender. A man who was betrayed by his wife—who took most of their property in the divorce and moved on with another man—concluded that **all women** were deceitful and untrustworthy. He began viewing all women through that **skewed lens** and raised his sons with that same distorted perspective. The damage this mentality causes is profound. It doesn't just harm the victim but can affect future generations and contribute to a **societal mindset** that perpetuates fear, distrust, and division.

3. Formation of Negative Attitudes

Narcissistic abuse has a lasting effect on a person's emotional health. It is often the root cause of **bitterness, hatred, unforgiveness**, and other destructive attitudes. The narcissist's goal is to tear down their victim's sense of **self-worth**—to make them feel inferior, insignificant, or undeserving of love and respect. This assault on their identity leaves deep emotional scars that are hard to heal. Victims often internalize these messages and start to view themselves as worthless or unworthy of happiness.

As a result, the pain and **humiliation** experienced in the relationship often manifest as negative emotions—**bitterness**, **resentment**, and **unforgiveness**. These feelings can become **entrenched** in the victim's heart and mind, shaping their future relationships and interactions with others. Without the proper tools to heal, these negative attitudes can become a permanent part of the person's emotional landscape, making it difficult to move forward.

How to Avoid Bleeding on Others

1. Take Full Control of Your Life

One of the most challenging aspects of healing from narcissistic abuse is breaking free from the emotional grip the abuser still has on you—even after the relationship has ended. Many victims continue to live under the shadow of the abuse, often internalizing their abuser's behaviors. They might start exhibiting narcissistic traits themselves, or they carry the burden of **bitterness** and **unforgiveness**. Others may unconsciously **transfer aggression** onto innocent people who had no part in their suffering.

These patterns are signs that you are **not fully in control** of your life or emotions.

The truth is, **bitterness** and **unforgiveness** do more harm to the victim than to the abuser. They trap you in the past, preventing you from moving forward. When you hold on to past pain, you lose the ability to fully engage with the present moment and experience the goodness around you.

No one, not even an abuser, should have that kind of control over your life.

The first step toward regaining control is **recognizing** that your emotions and reactions should not be dictated by someone else's behavior. Let go of the memories of the past, release the **bitterness**, and choose to **embrace forgiveness**. This doesn't mean excusing the abuse, but it's about reclaiming your peace and breaking free from the emotional chains that hold you back.

2. Think of Yourself in the Right Proportion
In Romans 12:3, the apostle Paul writes,
"For I say, through the grace given to me, to every one of you, not to think of himself more highly than he ought to think..."

This is an essential principle in countering the narcissistic tendencies that might have been internalized during abuse. Narcissism, at its core, stems from an **overestimation of one's self-importance**. This inflated sense of superiority is what causes individuals to disregard the feelings of others and manipulate situations for personal gain.

When victims of narcissistic abuse do not heal, they sometimes internalize these traits. They may start seeing themselves through the same distorted lens as their abuser—thinking their needs, desires, or opinions are more important than those of others.

To prevent this, it's crucial to **cultivate humility** and a **realistic self-assessment**. Think of yourself in **appropriate proportion**—recognizing your worth, but also acknowledging your imperfections and the importance of those around you. This practice of humility helps curb the self-centeredness that is a hallmark of narcissism, allowing you to rebuild your sense of self without the distortion that abuse causes.

3. Practice Empathy

A lack of empathy is one of the core traits of a narcissist. Narcissists not only exalt themselves above others but also **disregard the feelings** and needs of those around them. Whether it's family, friends, or colleagues, narcissists tend to view others as tools to serve their own desires, rather than as people with their own emotions and needs.

This lack of concern for others is what makes narcissism so damaging, both to individuals and society as a whole. While it might be excusable, though not ideal, for someone to overlook the feelings of a stranger, it becomes deeply troubling when it's someone close to you—someone you should care about and respect.

One of the most powerful ways to **break free from the cycle of narcissistic behavior** is to actively **practice empathy**. Empathy helps you connect with the feelings of others, fostering genuine care and consideration. By consistently considering the impact of your actions on those around you, you prevent the self-centeredness of narcissism from taking root in your own heart.

Empathy teaches you to balance your sense of self-importance with a genuine concern for others. Over time, it helps you rebuild healthy relationships and develop a more **balanced, compassionate** view of the world.

CHAPTER 3

Welcome to freedom

Some wounds are so deep that healing cannot be accomplished through our own efforts alone. In these moments of pain and despair, turning to the Lord becomes not just essential, but life changing. Only God has the power to heal the most profound emotional scars and restore true peace. He is the One who can mend even the most broken hearts, offering a comfort that transcends all understanding—a peace that endures beyond the hurt.

The Bible reminds us that God specializes in binding up the brokenhearted. This is particularly true for those who have suffered emotional trauma from narcissistic abuse. Narcissists leave a unique kind of scar on the soul, one that deeply impacts the heart and shapes how we view ourselves and others. For many, the emotional toll of being with a narcissist can fundamentally change who they are.

By the time some people come out of a relationship with a narcissist, they are no longer the person they once were. They may feel as though they've lost a part of themselves in the process. For some, the hurt manifests as a deep **hatred** or **disillusionment** toward the opposite sex—particularly among those who had narcissistic spouses or partners. After enduring manipulation, control, and emotional abuse, they may begin to see every one of the opposite sex through the same lens, as potential manipulators or abusers. The scars left behind by the narcissist cloud their perception of all relationships, creating a deep mistrust that's difficult to overcome.

This is not just about the breakdown of trust—it's the **conditioning of the heart**. The pain of betrayal can leave a person feeling emotionally **shackled**, unable to move forward without bitterness or fear. For some, this results in a hardened heart, filled with **vengeance** or an **unforgiving spirit**. The anger and resentment they carry are a direct result of the wounds inflicted during the narcissistic relationship.

These are emotional **tight corners**—places so painful and difficult to escape that they feel suffocating. It's easy to feel trapped in a cycle of hurt, unable to move forward or heal on your own. But here's the truth: **you do not have to do it alone**. God's grace is more than sufficient to break these chains.

God has a way of reaching into the deepest parts of our hearts, healing the wounds we thought could never be healed, and restoring what was broken. He can soften the hardest of hearts, replacing bitterness with forgiveness and healing the deepest emotional scars with His love. It is in His presence that true freedom is found—the kind of freedom that doesn't just release you from the grip of narcissistic abuse but also sets you free from the emotional baggage that abuse leaves behind.

With God's help, healing becomes possible. Through His grace, you can reclaim your peace, regain trust in others, and rediscover a sense of hope and joy that seemed lost forever. Welcome to the freedom that only God can provide.

Receive God's Help

God is always ready and willing to help us with any challenge or hardship we face. However, His help comes on His terms, not ours. To receive God's healing and restoration, we must align ourselves with His requirements. The good news is that God's requirements are never burdensome or difficult to follow. In fact, they lead to true freedom and peace.

1 John 5:3
"For this is the love of God, that we keep His commandments: and His commandments are not grievous."

The first step in receiving God's help is to **surrender** to Him. This means letting go of any pain, bitterness, or anger you may be holding onto. **Release**

the hurt from your heart, and trust that God is capable of healing even the deepest wounds.

Don't allow bitterness to cloud your heart or drive you toward seeking revenge. Instead, trust God to handle matters on your behalf. He promises that vengeance belongs to Him.

Romans 12:19
"Dearly beloved, avenge not yourselves, but rather give place unto wrath: for it is written, Vengeance is mine; I will repay, saith the Lord."

When you surrender your hurt and your desire for revenge to God, it signals to Him that you **trust His judgment**. It demonstrates that you **rely on His faithfulness** to bring justice and healing in His perfect timing. Let go of the need to control the situation and allow God to handle it according to His will.

On the other hand, when we try to take matters into our own hands and act out of our own power, we essentially tell God, "I don't trust You to handle this." This is not the posture of someone who is ready to receive God's help. It's impossible to experience God's restoration if we are not willing to let go of control and place our trust fully in Him.

To receive God's help, you must first surrender your heart and your will to Him. **Release your burdens, forgive those who have hurt you, and trust that He will bring about justice in His time.** When you do this, you open yourself to the full extent of His healing power, knowing that His plans for you are always good.

Coming Under God's System of Forgiveness

In my book *Moving Past the Hurt*, I discuss how God's system of forgiveness is vastly different from the world's approach. It's a system that requires those who seek His help to fully embrace it. Forgiveness, as outlined in Scripture, is not always easy, but it is always necessary for healing and freedom.

In one of the most well-known conversations between Peter and Jesus, Peter asks how many times he should forgive someone who wrongs him. He wonders, "Lord, how often shall I forgive someone who sins against me? Up to seven times?" (Matthew 18:21). Jesus responds with something truly shocking: "I tell you, not seven times, but seventy-seven times" (or in some translations, "seventy times seven" – 490 times).

Peter must have been stunned. I know I would have been! It's hard to imagine forgiving someone that many times, especially if they continuously hurt you. Peter, probably thinking of someone who had been irritating him endlessly, was likely hoping for a number that would give him permission to finally give that person a piece of his mind, or maybe even cut them off entirely. But Jesus' response was radical and challenging.

What Jesus was teaching isn't just about counting offenses, but about adopting a **posture of forgiveness**. The 490 times is symbolic; it's not about literally keeping a tally of every offense. Rather, it's about forgiving ahead of time, not letting offense take root in our hearts at all. You can't possibly keep track of the 200th or 300th wrong—if you are truly practicing forgiveness, you let go of offense **before** it even has the chance to take hold.

This is where we often struggle. Our natural inclination is to hold on to offense, especially when we feel that the person who wronged us doesn't "deserve" our forgiveness. In many cases they may not, but God's call to forgive isn't about whether or not they deserve it. **His forgiveness is about obedience to His commands and protecting your own heart.**

God's system of forgiveness is designed to protect us from the devastating effects of holding on to offense. The longer we carry that burden, the more it poisons our hearts. Offense and unforgiveness distort our thinking and rob us of peace. **The danger of offense is largely on the person who holds it**, not the person who caused the offense.

Think about this: if God were to keep track of all our wrongdoings toward Him, our list would far outweigh the wrongs of anyone who ever hurt us. Yet

God, in His mercy, forgives us over and over, and He asks us to do the same with others. **Forgiveness isn't about the other person deserving it—it's about following God's example of grace and mercy.** When we choose to forgive, we are not just obeying a command, but we are also choosing to free ourselves from the chains of bitterness and resentment.

Forgiving others may seem impossible in some situations, but when we understand that forgiveness is not for the offender's sake but for ours, it becomes a lot clearer. God's system of forgiveness protects us, heals us, and restores peace to our hearts.

Seventh Column; Closing the Backdoor

The term "seventh column" comes from military terminology used during World War II. It was associated with the unintended damage caused by negligence and carelessness within a military force. While the "fifth column" referred to enemy spies and saboteurs infiltrating from within, and the "sixth column" was the group of people aiding them, the "seventh column" referred to the internal dangers caused by carelessness, unawareness, or failure to maintain vigilance, which could weaken a country's defenses just as much as an external attack.

In the spiritual realm, a similar principle applies. As human beings, we must be aware that there are spiritual forces—demonic spirits—that seek to infiltrate our lives and wreak havoc. These spirits often gain access through moments of unguarded vulnerability, especially when we are not vigilant. Certain behaviors or attitudes can act as "backdoors," opening us up to these negative influences.

Things like **anger, bitterness, unforgiveness**, and other harmful emotions can serve as openings, inviting spiritual attacks or creating footholds for demonic oppression. When we hold on to these feelings, we unwittingly grant the enemy a "place" in our lives.

The Bible clearly addresses this danger in Ephesians 4:26-27: *"Be angry and do not sin; do not let the sun go down on your anger and give no opportunity to the devil."*

Even though emotions like anger and unforgiveness can sometimes feel justified—especially in response to past hurts, particularly from toxic relationships like those with narcissists—**they still expose us to spiritual danger**. These emotions, left unchecked, can turn into **strongholds**—areas of our lives where the enemy gains control, causing long-term damage to our emotional, mental, and spiritual well-being.

For many victims of narcissistic abuse, these fleshly reactions—anger, bitterness, unforgiveness—are often natural responses to the trauma they've endured. However, these reactions can also become entry points for spiritual oppression. When someone is hurt repeatedly, especially by someone they trusted, it's easy to become trapped in these negative emotions. **But it's crucial to recognize that these feelings, while understandable, can lead to greater spiritual harm if left unchecked.**

As we deal with past hurts, it's essential to understand that, in God's eyes, **holding onto unforgiveness or bitterness is not just a personal matter**—it's a spiritual issue that can have serious consequences. It can open doors for spiritual forces to exploit our pain, keeping us trapped in cycles of emotional turmoil and spiritual weakness.

Closing the backdoor to these spiritual threats requires intentional effort: letting go of anger, embracing forgiveness, and allowing God to heal the wounds of the past. When we choose to release bitterness and unforgiveness, we effectively close those openings and regain control of our spiritual lives. In doing so, we protect ourselves from the internal "weakness" that can be just as dangerous as any external attack.

Dealing with the Spirit of Unforgiveness

Unforgiveness often starts as a natural, human response to hurt or injustice, rooted in the flesh. However, if it is not dealt with, it quickly evolves into something much more dangerous. What begins as an emotional reaction can soon become an **open door** for demonic forces, turning what was once a mere response to pain into a **demonic stronghold**.

At this point, unforgiveness is no longer just a matter of personal bitterness; it has become a **full-blown spiritual operation**. The spirit of unforgiveness partners with **bitterness** to harden the heart, making forgiveness seem impossible. It distorts your thoughts, influencing you to cling to offense, and pushes you to go against God's commands to hold onto your anger. It entices you to forfeit your peace of mind and joy to preserve the right to remain bitter.

A person under the influence of this spirit is often trapped in **perpetual frustration**. There is a constant undercurrent of tension and unrest, which prevents true peace from taking root in their heart. Unforgiveness brings spiritual and emotional chaos, undermining their well-being and peace.

What makes this spirit even more insidious is its ultimate goal: it's not actually targeting the person who wronged you, but rather **seeking to destroy you**. The demonic spirit behind unforgiveness aims to **steal your joy**, **rob you of peace**, and **hinder your relationship with God**. It feeds off your pain, pushing you further into isolation and torment.

This is why it is crucial to **resist the spirit of unforgiveness**—not just for your own emotional healing, but for your spiritual freedom. In the name of Jesus, you can break the chains of unforgiveness. You have the authority to reject bitterness and choose forgiveness, which is the only true path to peace and healing.

Remember, unforgiveness is a trap set by the enemy, but with God's help, you can overcome it and reclaim the joy and peace that belong to you.

Deliverance From the Spirit of Unforgiveness

Isaiah 49:24-25:

"Shall the prey be taken from the mighty, or the lawful captive delivered? But thus saith the Lord, Even the captives of the mighty shall be taken away, and the prey of the terrible shall be delivered: for I will contend with him that contendeth with thee..."

James 4:7:

"Submit yourselves therefore to God. Resist the devil, and he will flee from you."

The path to deliverance from the spirit of unforgiveness begins with a **declaration of authority** in the name of Jesus. Your first step is to **cast out** that demonic spirit from your life and affairs. This is a privilege and right of every believer who has accepted Jesus Christ as Lord and Savior.

Once you've done that, don't worry about whether the spirits will leave or not—**declare in the name of Jesus** that they must go. Demons cannot withstand the power of His name, and they will flee when you command them to leave. Stand firm in your authority and trust that **they must go.**

However, deliverance doesn't stop with casting out the demonic spirit; the next crucial step is **renewing your mind. Romans 12:1-2** instructs us to not only present our bodies as living sacrifices to God, but also to be transformed by the **renewing of our minds**. Deliverance is incomplete until the mind has been renewed, because demons work to influence your thoughts and keep you in patterns that align with their evil desires. They seek to **conform your mind** to their lies, keeping you trapped in unforgiveness.

To experience complete transformation, you must expose your mind to **God's Word**—the truth that breaks every chain. Find and meditate on Scripture that speaks to the power of forgiveness, healing, and deliverance. The more you immerse yourself in God's truth, the stronger your mind becomes in resisting the enemy's attempts to reassert control.

It's important to know that the demonic spirit will **fight** to regain control of your mind. It will try to bring thoughts of offense and bitterness back to the surface. But your role is to continue resisting the enemy—stand firm in your faith, and **he will flee**.

1 Peter 5:9 tells us to resist the devil, "steadfast in the faith." As you continue to renew your mind, fill your heart with God's truth, and stand firm in your authority in Christ, you will experience the **freedom and peace** that come from a life free of unforgiveness.

Remember, **deliverance is a process**, but with God's help, it is a process that leads to lasting freedom. Continue resisting, continue renewing, and continue relying on God's Word to bring complete healing.

Dealing with the Spirit of Hatred

I've heard stories of women who, after leaving toxic marriages, allowed the pain and trauma they suffered to fuel a deep hatred towards the opposite sex. In some cases, this unresolved pain manifests in campaigns against men and the traditional role of headship in the home. Unfortunately, these women did not receive the healing they desperately needed, and as a result, their negative experiences transformed into a bitterness that taints their view of all men.

Similarly, I've listened to the stories of men who were severely hurt by relationships with women—some losing their properties, careers, children, and businesses. Instead of seeking healing through God's grace, they allowed the bitterness from their past experiences to morph into a deep-seated hatred for women. Beyond physical attraction, they began to see no value in women and, in doing so, shut themselves off from the many blessings that God has placed within them.

Both of these examples reflect the danger of unresolved pain turning into **hatred**, which opens the door for demonic spirits to enter. A person who operates in hatred, whether towards men or women, creates a spiritual opening that the enemy can exploit. This allows these spirits to amplify their bitterness and intensify their hatred, pushing them further away from God's healing and peace.

The longer someone walks in hatred, the more they become susceptible to spiritual influence that fuels this destructive emotion. Hatred is not just an emotional response—it is a spirit that can grow stronger if left unchecked. Without the intervention of God's healing power, these negative emotions can spiral, affecting not only their relationships but their entire lives.

The only way to break free from this cycle is to allow God to heal the wounds that caused the hatred in the first place. When we surrender our pain to God and trust in His ability to heal our hearts, we can find freedom from the grip of hatred and begin to see others through His eyes, filled with grace and love.

Deliverance from the Spirit of Hatred

Isaiah 49:24-25:

"Shall the prey be taken from the mighty, or the lawful captive delivered? But thus saith the Lord: Even the captives of the mighty shall be taken away, and the prey of the terrible shall be delivered; for I will contend with him that contends with thee, and I will save thy children."

The first step in your self-deliverance from the grip of demonic spirits is to cast them out of your life and affairs in the name of Jesus. This is the exclusive right of every believer who has given their life to Jesus.

Once you declare in Jesus' name, do not worry whether the demonic spirits will leave. The name of Jesus has authority over all spiritual forces, and they cannot stand against the power of His name. Simply declare your freedom, and trust that they must flee.

However, deliverance is not complete until there is a **renewal of the mind**. Demons work to program a person's mind, influencing their thoughts and behaviors to continue doing their bidding. This is why transformation must come from God's Word.

Romans 12:1-2 says:

"I beseech you therefore, brethren, by the mercies of God, that ye present your

bodies a living sacrifice, holy, acceptable unto God, which is your reasonable service. And be not conformed to this world: but be ye transformed by the renewing of your mind, that ye may prove what is that good, and acceptable, and perfect, will of God."

The renewal of your mind happens when you intentionally expose your thoughts to God's Word. Specifically, meditate on scriptural passages that address issues like unforgiveness, bitterness, and healing. As you do this, you are renewing your mind and aligning it with God's truth.

The demonic spirits will try to fight back, attempting to regain control of your thoughts and emotions. But you must resist them continually. Keep standing firm in God's Word, and as you do, the enemy will flee. Your freedom comes when you hold fast to the truth that in Christ, you are delivered and made new.

CHAPTER 4

Shining like a star

One of the most profound issues faced by victims of narcissistic abuse is the loss of identity. Narcissists thrive on diminishing others to inflate their own egos and pride, and over time, their victims internalize this devaluation. This constant undermining erodes a person's sense of self-worth, often leaving them with low self-esteem and confusion about who they truly are.

A person who is continually ridiculed or belittled begins to lose confidence in themselves. The narcissist's tactics of manipulation and emotional control not only leave their victims feeling less than they are, but also create a false narrative in their minds. The more someone is subjected to this toxic behavior, the more they start to question their value and their place in the world.

At the core of human interactions is **identity**. It's the reason we have names, the foundation of how we connect with others and understand our purpose in life. When a person's identity is unclear or compromised, they start living beneath their potential, unable to grasp their true worth.

There is a story of a lion cub that illustrates this point perfectly. A farmer found the cub seriously injured and near death. The compassionate farmer took the cub in and cared for it, placing it among his flock of sheep. As the lion cub grew, it lived and interacted with the sheep, eating, playing, and resting alongside them. Over time, the cub began to take on the behavior of the sheep, losing its natural instincts and identity as the king of the jungle.

When the lion cub went out with the sheep, it would run in fear at the sight of any predator, just like the sheep did. The cub, once destined to rule the jungle and feared by all, had now become a timid, frightened creature, constantly living in fear. It had forgotten who it truly was and began to live beneath its rightful nature.

Then, one day, a lion appeared near the farmer's home. It roared loudly, sending the sheep into a panic, and even the lion cub ran in terror. A few days later, the cub wandered to a river and saw its own reflection in the water. For a moment, it froze, thinking it had encountered the very lion that had frightened them earlier. It ran for cover, confused and frightened, unaware that the reflection was its own image. The sheep, however, remained unphased, because they did not recognize the lion cub as anything other than one of their own.

A few days later, the lion cub saw its reflection again in the river, this time with a growing sense of awareness. As it looked into the water, it began to recognize something stirring inside of it. At that moment, the older lion—the one that had frightened the sheep—emerged from the bushes. As the lion approached, it made a powerful roar, one that resonated deep within the cub. Something awakened inside the cub. It wasn't just a sound—it was a call to action. The cub, surprised and intrigued, found itself mimicking the roar. For the first time, it realized its true identity.

No longer did it see itself as one of the sheep. It had always been a lion, but it had lost sight of that truth. The older lion encouraged the cub to follow, and without hesitation, the cub decided to step into its true identity. It followed the older lion back into the jungle, no longer hiding, no longer living in fear.

Just like the lion cub, many victims of narcissism lose sight of their true identity. They are manipulated, devalued, and conditioned to live beneath their worth. But when they begin to recognize the truth about who they are—when they come to understand that they are made for more than the abuse they've endured—they can step into the fullness of their potential and reclaim their lives.

The journey to healing and reclaiming your identity may take time, but it begins with recognizing that you were never meant to live in fear or beneath your worth. You are not defined by the abuse you've experienced. Your true identity is not shaped by the lies of a narcissist, but by the truth of who you are in Christ. Like the lion cub, you have the power to awaken to your true nature, and once you do, there is nothing that can hold you back from living the life you were meant to lead.

Blurry and Distorted Identity

There are several factors that can negatively impact a person's sense of identity, causing it to either become blurry or completely distorted. A blurry identity occurs when a person starts to lose clarity about who they are and what their true purpose is. In contrast, a distorted identity refers to a scenario where someone has an image of themselves, but that image is warped—diminished and stripped of the inherent value they possess. In this case, the person's true brilliance and potential are masked by inaccurate perceptions shaped by external influences.

Three prominent factors often contribute to this blurry or distorted image:

1. **Toxic Relationship** with a Narcissist
2. **Negative Circumstances** or Experiences
3. **Satanic Attack**

1. Toxic Relationship with a Narcissist

Relationships with narcissists can have devastating effects on a person's identity. Narcissists thrive on diminishing others to inflate their own egos, and their manipulative behaviors can leave deep emotional scars. As previously discussed, a narcissist constantly belittles others, often in subtle and insidious ways. Over time, this relentless negativity erodes the victim's self-esteem and can lead them to internalize the false narrative their abuser has created.

Consider the case of a woman who was repeatedly labeled a "doormat" and a "simpleton" by her narcissistic husband. Over time, these cruel labels began to shape her self-image. Once a highly competent accountant, she began to doubt her abilities and started seeing herself through the distorted lens her husband had created. The more she internalized these negative labels, the more her confidence eroded. She started to behave in ways that mirrored the traits she had been accused of.

Such sustained toxicity not only damages emotional well-being but can also fundamentally alter one's sense of self. When this happens, the victim may struggle to reclaim their true identity, having been led to believe they are less than they really are.

2. Negative Circumstances or Experiences

When a person is faced with prolonged negative circumstances, they may begin to define themselves by those circumstances. Take, for instance, the case of a beautiful, smart, and godly young woman who had been hoping for marriage but had yet to find a partner. Over time, she began to question her worth. If she was truly as valuable as she once believed, she reasoned, someone should have pursued her by now. She started seeing her prolonged singleness as a reflection of her own inadequacy. Her once-healthy self-esteem began to erode, and she began to project her "failure" in this area onto her entire life.

Soon, she started living out of this distorted image. A promising young woman, full of potential, started to carry herself like someone rejected or unwanted. Her circumstances had become her identity, and she allowed them to define her in a way that was neither true nor fair.

Royalty Became a Dead Dog

There is a story in the Bible that beautifully illustrates how negative circumstances can distort a person's identity. Mephibosheth, the grandson of King Saul, was once a member of Israel's royal family. However, a tragic accident left him lame and unable to walk, and his life took a turn for the worse. When news of the death of Saul and Jonathan reached him, his nurse fled in panic, and in the chaos, Mephibosheth fell, leaving him permanently disabled.

As a result of this injury, Mephibosheth was forced to live in hiding. He became disconnected from his royal roots, and his identity as a member of the royal family was lost. By the time David, the new king of Israel, sought to show kindness to Saul's descendants, Mephibosheth had been living in obscurity. His circumstances—his disability, isolation, and suffering—had so deeply affected him that he saw himself as less than nothing.

When Mephibosheth finally came before King David, he referred to himself as "a dead dog"—a complete rejection of his true identity as a prince. He had internalized his suffering and felt utterly unworthy of the king's kindness.

2 Samuel 9:6-8: *"When Mephibosheth, the son of Jonathan, the son of Saul, came to David, he fell on his face to the ground in reverence. 'Mephibosheth,' David said, 'Your servant!' 'Do not be afraid,' David said to him, 'for I will surely show you kindness for the sake of your father Jonathan. I will restore to you all the land that belonged to your grandfather Saul, and you will always eat at my table.' Mephibosheth bowed down and said, 'What is your servant, that you should notice a dead dog like me?'"*

Mephibosheth's circumstances had clouded his identity, but David saw him for who he truly was—a prince with a rightful place at the king's table. He had allowed negative experiences to define him, but David's kindness helped him rediscover his true identity.

3. Satanic Attack

Satan is a master manipulator, skilled at using negative circumstances to bind a person to a false identity. When a person faces a persistent challenge or affliction—such as infertility, financial struggles, or chronic illness—Satan will often amplify the emotional toll, pushing them to see themselves as defined by that issue.

For instance, consider a couple who struggled for years with infertility. Over time, the intensity of their situation caused them to focus on their inability to conceive. The wife, who had once been a confident and successful individual, began to identify herself as "barren." Despite her many accomplishments, she started to view herself as a failure because of her struggle with infertility.

This is how Satan works—he isolates a single issue, amplifies it, and causes a person to define their entire worth around that one problem. He seeks to lock people into false identities that keep them from walking in the fullness of their potential.

Reclaiming Your True Identity
Each of these factors—**toxic relationships, negative circumstances**, and **satanic manipulation**—has the power to cloud and distort the image a person holds of themselves. They may lead you to live beneath your true worth and potential. However, **the good news** is that your true identity is not defined by the circumstances or people around you.

Like Mephibosheth, you may have lived with a distorted image of who you are, but it's time to stop living under the weight of negative experiences and rediscover your true identity. You are not a "dead dog" or a "failure" or defined by any setback. You are made in the image of God, and His truth about you is far more powerful than any lie that has been spoken over you.

Reclaiming your true identity begins with a decision to reject the lies and embrace the truth of who you are in Christ. You were created with purpose, equipped with gifts, and called to live a life of greatness. No circumstance or label can take that away. It's time to see yourself as God sees you—redeemed, loved, and destined for greatness.

Breaking the Bond of Blurry and Distorted Image

Your true identity is found in Christ and in the eternal truths He speaks over you. These words are far superior to any negative label, opinion, or experience that you may have encountered. In Christ, you find the reality of who you truly are, not the distorted version shaped by your past wounds or toxic relationships.

Even when your true identity feels clouded, when your self-worth seems to be slipping away, the word of God has the power to reveal your true self—an image created by God, not by the circumstances that have tried to define you.

When You Feel Worthless

When the world or your circumstances make you feel insignificant or unworthy, the truth in God's word tells you the opposite:

"I will praise thee; for I am fearfully and wonderfully made: marvelous are thy works; and that my soul knoweth right well."
— **Psalm 139:14**

This verse affirms that you are not just a random creation, but a purposeful and beautifully made person. No matter what negative experiences or people have said about you, God's truth stands stronger: **you are fearfully and wonderfully made.**

When You Feel Rejected

When rejection from others has you questioning your value, God's love remains constant:

"Can a woman forget her sucking child, that she should not have compassion on the son of her womb? Yea, they may forget, yet will I not forget thee. Behold, I have graven thee upon the palms of my hands; thy walls are continually before me."
— **Isaiah 49:15-16**

God's love for you is unshakable. Even if people abandon or neglect you, God promises never to forget you. You are always in His thoughts, and your worth is engraved on His hands. His love for you is permanent, and it transcends all the rejection you may have faced.

When You Feel Hopeless

When you feel like all hope is lost and you want to give up, God's word reminds you of His plans for you:

"For I know the plans I have for you," declares the Lord, "plans to prosper you and not to harm you, plans to give you a hope and a future."
— **Jeremiah 29:11** (NIV)

Even in your lowest moments, God has a plan for you—a plan filled with hope and a future. This truth can guide you out of despair and back to the purpose God has for your life. No matter how grim the situation may seem, God is at work to bring you to a place of healing, restoration, and fulfillment.

The Power of Your Choice
You have the power to choose which identity you will embrace. Will you allow your circumstances, past hurts, and the lies of others define you? Or will you choose to stand firm on the truth of God's Word, which says that you are **fearfully and wonderfully made** and **treasured by God**?

It's essential to make the choice to embrace your true identity in Christ, despite all the odds. The enemy will try to pull you back into negative thinking—thoughts that diminish your worth. But you have the power to resist those lies by consistently aligning your thoughts with God's truth.

Silence the Negative Thoughts with God's Word
The enemy will attempt to replay the painful memories of your past, trying to convince you that you are still the person your experiences have made you. He'll whisper that you're weak, that you're worthless, that you'll never change. But God's Word is the antidote to those lies. You must replace those negative thoughts with the truth of who God says you are.

Studies have shown that prolonged exposure to narcissistic abuse, emotional manipulation, or any form of toxic relationship can drastically reshape the victim's perception of themselves. The longer someone stays trapped in the mud of hurt, the more likely they are to start seeing themselves as inferior or unworthy. If you've been hurt by a narcissist, you may have started to think that something is wrong with you, or that you aren't good enough. These lies can invade your thoughts and distort your sense of self.

The Dangers of Negative Conditioning
When you allow these thoughts to linger—when you begin to accept them as truths—it can lead you to make choices that reinforce these distorted views of yourself. You might begin doing things that diminish your worth, simply

to seek validation or acceptance from others. This is the danger of negative conditioning.

But the antidote to this is **to start seeing yourself the way God sees you.**

God is the only one who has an accurate picture of your true identity. Unlike the false perceptions formed by your painful experiences or the lies you've believed, God created you with intention, purpose, and beauty. You are **not a mistake**, nor are you trash—**you are a treasure.**

God's View of You

Even when past mistakes have left scars, or when others have made you feel small, remember that you were **fearfully and wonderfully made.** Your value is not determined by your failures or your pain. God created you with incredible potential to make wise, loving choices. You were designed to fulfill a unique purpose on this earth.

God's intention for your life is not defined by your past hurt, but by His love and purpose for you.

You are a masterpiece, not a mistake. God does not create junk—He creates masterpieces. And you, regardless of the circumstances in your life, are His masterpiece. You were created for something extremely significant. Your worth cannot be defined by others' opinions or by the wounds of the past. It is defined by God, who knows the plans He has for you—a future filled with hope and purpose.

Made in the Image of God

In the natural world, everything reproduces after its own kind. Humans give birth to humans, animals to animals, and you will never find a coconut growing on a mango tree. This law of nature demonstrates that each kind reflects its origin.

The same principle applies to you: **You were created in the image of God.** This is a powerful truth that should fill you with pride, not arrogance, but a deep sense of value. Being made in God's image means that you share similarities with God. **God is full of glory; you are a glorious being.** Regardless of what circumstances or negative experiences have led you to believe about yourself, your true nature is one of radiating glory because that is the essence of who you are.

The problem is that, often due to ignorance or painful experiences, many people fail to see their true worth. It's like a lion cub thinking it's a rat simply because of some unfavorable circumstances. But **your identity is not defined by your circumstances.** Circumstances are just events—they do not dictate who you are. Your identity is rooted in your origin. **You were made in the image of God.** That is the truest and most accurate reflection of who you are.

You Are More Than You Think
You are not just a random being living on earth. You are **You**—a special creation of God, uniquely designed by Him for a purpose far greater than you can imagine. You are **saved by the precious blood of Jesus**, which means you are immeasurably valuable. God takes a personal, deep interest in you and everything concerning you. **You are more than you think**—far more than the world or your past circumstances have led you to believe.

If you have experienced narcissistic abuse or any form of emotional manipulation, it can be difficult to see yourself as valuable. These experiences can distort your sense of self-worth and leave you feeling small or insignificant. But you must **reconfigure your mind**—begin to believe that you are more than your past and more than what those negative experiences have tried to make you think. The truth is, **God would not pay special attention to you if you were not worth it.**

God, in His majesty and greatness, **created you in His own image**. This is priceless. This is why it is so important to **remind yourself constantly** that you are made in His image. **You are His masterpiece.**

The Dangers of Low Self-Worth

Having low self-worth can keep you trapped in a cycle of depression, self-pity, and fear. When you believe you are not valuable, it holds you back from pursuing your dreams, trying new things, and stepping out of your comfort zone. People with low self-worth tend to have an inferiority complex and a constant feeling of inadequacy, which makes them vulnerable to being manipulated by narcissists and toxic people.

But you **must never** allow low self-worth to dominate your life. I know that narcissistic abuse or difficult experiences may have conditioned you to think less of yourself, but it's crucial to **work on reclaiming your true worth.** God wants you to recognize your value, because **you are invaluable** in His eyes.

Your Past Does Not Define Your Value

Knowing your true worth will help you understand that **your past experiences do not diminish your value.** Whatever you have gone through, no matter how painful, does not reduce who you are. Your worth is defined by **the precious blood of Jesus**, and nothing can take that value away.

You were created by God, and He doesn't make mistakes. Your value is incredibly high—so high, in fact, that God sent His Son to die for you. This is the value you carry, and it doesn't change based on what others have said or done to you.

A Journey to Self-Discovery

Now is the time for you to **embark on a journey of self-discovery.** Begin to explore who you truly are in Christ, beyond the lies and labels that have been placed on you. The abuse or hurt you've experienced does not define you—it is only part of your story, not the whole story.

Take time to understand and embrace the truth that you are **God's masterpiece**, uniquely created for a purpose. Let go of the false beliefs that a narcissist or anyone else may have instilled in you. You were created with inherent worth and dignity, and **that will never change.**

It's time to step into the fullness of who you are in Christ. You are more than enough. You are **fearfully and wonderfully made**—and this truth will always stand, no matter what you've been through or what anyone else has said. Begin to walk in the knowledge of your true identity, and let your life reflect the glory of the One who created you.

1. Discover Your True Value

When the value of something is not recognized, it is easily underpriced. Similarly, if you don't understand your own worth, it becomes harder for others to see it. When you discover your true value and present yourself accordingly, people will treat you with the respect and honor you deserve. This process of self-discovery is vital for shaping your self-image and understanding your worth.

Feeling sorry for yourself is a sure way to remain stagnant. You'll stay stuck in the same place while the world continues to move forward. Self-pity clouds your judgment and prevents you from seeing your true value. It convinces you that you're incapable of achieving anything or making progress. When you know your worth, you naturally exude a confidence that empowers you to take action and embrace opportunities.

Do not allow the hurt from narcissistic abuse to lower your self-esteem or make you timid. **You are valuable.** Recognize it. Replace the feeling of self-pity with confidence and self-assurance. **You are worth more than the hurt you've endured**, and when you understand that others will treat you as such.

2. Discover Your Potential and Gifts

Each person has unique potential and gifts, and these were given to you by God. You have talents, abilities, and a purpose that are uniquely yours, and they were entrusted to you because God sees you as worthy. **Your gifts are not random or insignificant**—they are carefully designed to fulfill a specific purpose in your life and in the lives of others. This is further proof that you were created with intention, and you are valuable in God's eyes.

Discovering your potential and talents will significantly boost your self-esteem and self-image. The more you uncover about your abilities, the more you'll see yourself as someone with purpose and importance. Look within yourself: **What are the things you enjoy doing?** Your hobbies and passions often align with your natural gifts. Spend time reflecting on what brings you joy and fulfillment—it's likely that these activities are connected to your greater potential.

3. Put Your Gifts to Good Use

Once you begin using your gifts and talents, you will find that you have less time to feel sorry for yourself. **Living a purposeful life brings fulfillment**, and fulfillment is a powerful antidote to low self-worth. The more you live according to your God-given purpose, the more confident you will become in your abilities and your worth. You'll gradually let go of the hurt and shift your focus to what you can create, achieve, and contribute to the world.

As you get busy embracing your purpose and using your gifts, the pain from your past will begin to fade. Over time, you will reach a place where the wounds of narcissistic abuse no longer control your identity. **You will hold your head high**, knowing that you are a person of immense value, worthy of love, respect, and success.

Your past experiences do not define you. **You are special**, designed by God with intentionality and love. You are **His masterpiece**. No one, not even a narcissist, has the power to change that. Reject any feelings of inferiority and discard the false beliefs that have been implanted in your mind. You are more than capable, and you deserve to live a life full of purpose, fulfillment, and joy.

In every step of your journey to rediscover your true identity, remember this: **You are valuable. You are worthy. You are loved by God, designed for greatness**, and nothing—no experience, no abusive relationship—can take that away. Embrace your true worth, cultivate your gifts, and step confidently into the life you were always meant to live.

CHAPTER 5
Overcoming Narcissism holds

Narcissists are master manipulators, and their tactics are designed to control and dominate their victims. Their behavior is rooted in manipulation and deceit, which can be considered a form of psychological control, often compared to basic witchcraft in its ability to affect a person's mind and emotions. Narcissistic abuse is profoundly damaging, so much so that anyone in their right mind would instinctively want to break free from it. However, narcissists know this, and they wield manipulation to tighten their grip and keep their victims trapped in their web of control.

Some of the most common narcissistic manipulation tactics include:

- Silent Treatment

- Gaslighting

- Narcissistic Rage

1. Silent Treatment

The silent treatment is one of the narcissist's go-to methods for exerting control. It is essentially a form of emotional punishment where the narcissist refuses to speak to you, often for extended periods. The goal of this tactic is to make you feel invisible, unimportant, or unworthy of their attention and affection.

While this tactic might be bearable in casual relationships, it becomes far more damaging when it comes from someone who is supposed to love and care for you—such as a spouse or close partner. Narcissists know that this will cause emotional turmoil and force their victims to seek their attention, which the narcissist uses to reassert control. The silent treatment is not about needing space or time to process emotions; it is about punishing you and making you feel unloved, so you become dependent on them for validation.

By refusing to engage, the narcissist forces you to chase after them, and in doing so, they manipulate your emotions to ensure that you continue to crave their approval. This keeps you on their emotional leash.

2. Gaslighting

Gaslighting is one of the most insidious forms of narcissistic manipulation. It involves making someone doubt their perception of reality, their memory, or even their sanity. Narcissists are experts at gaslighting, and they use it to confuse their victims and make them question what they know to be true.

A narcissist may accuse you of things that they themselves are guilty of, or they may twist situations so that you end up apologizing when, in fact, you were the one wronged. They will constantly shift the blame onto you, deflecting responsibility for their own actions and causing you to second-guess your judgment. This tactic is particularly dangerous because it erodes your self-confidence, leaving you more vulnerable to their control.

For example, a narcissist might accuse you of being forgetful when they were the one who failed to keep their promises. Or, they might deny something they said or did, causing you to doubt your memory and eventually apologize for something that wasn't your fault. Over time, this consistent manipulation undermines your trust in yourself, making it easier for the narcissist to manipulate you further.

3. Narcissistic Rage

Narcissistic rage is often disproportionate to the actual event that triggered it, but it is a powerful tool for manipulating and intimidating victims. This kind of rage is unpredictable, and it often comes out of nowhere, leaving you confused and fearful. The narcissist might explode with anger over something trivial, but their reaction is deliberately designed to make you feel fearful and submissive.

A narcissist uses rage to reassert dominance. They will belittle, insult, or verbally attack their victim to restore control and make them feel small and helpless. The narcissist's anger is rarely about the issue at hand—it's about instilling fear and ensuring that you stay in a subservient position. When confronted, a narcissist will often escalate their anger, using personal insults or threats to intimidate you into submission. This creates an atmosphere of constant tension, where you're always walking on eggshells, unsure of when the next outburst will occur.

The goal of narcissistic rage is to break your spirit and force you to accept the narcissist's narrative, making you feel that you are always to blame or responsible for their outbursts. In the aftermath, the narcissist may act as though nothing happened, or they may try to manipulate you into feeling guilty for "provoking" them. This pattern of emotional abuse is designed to break your will and keep you emotionally entangled with the narcissist.

Overcoming the Hold of Narcissistic Abuse

Breaking free from the emotional manipulation of a narcissist is challenging, but it is possible. The first step is recognizing these tactics for what they are: tools of control and power. Narcissists thrive on keeping their victims in a state of confusion, self-doubt, and emotional dependency. To overcome these holds, you must begin to:

1. **Recognize the Manipulation** – Understanding that the narcissist's behavior is not your fault is crucial. Their tactics are designed to confuse and control you, not because you deserve to be treated this way, but because they seek power over you.

2. **Set Boundaries** – Narcissists push boundaries, but you must learn to set healthy emotional boundaries that protect you from their manipulation. Refuse to tolerate the silent treatment, gaslighting, or rage. Stand firm in your sense of self-worth.

3. **Strengthen Your Self-Worth** – Narcissists want to tear down your self-esteem, but by recognizing your inherent value and purpose, you can regain your sense of self. Remind yourself that you are worthy of love, respect, and healthy relationships.

4. **Seek Support** – Don't try to face narcissistic abuse alone. Find support from trusted friends, family, or professionals who understand the dynamics of narcissistic manipulation. You don't have to suffer in silence.

5. **Take Back Your Power** – Once you recognize the tactics and reclaim your self-worth, you can begin to take control of your own life again. This may involve distancing yourself from the narcissist, whether physically or emotionally, and reclaiming your sense of peace.

Narcissistic abuse is insidious, but it is not permanent. With time, support, and a commitment to healing, you can overcome the manipulation and restore your true sense of self. You were never meant to live under the control of anyone—especially not someone who seeks to tear you down. Your identity and value are defined by God, not by the narcissist's lies. Stand firm in that truth and begin the journey to reclaim your life.

How to Handle Narcissistic Abuse in Some Relationships

1. Boss-Employee Relationship

A. Broaden Your Network

In a challenging boss-employee relationship, particularly with a narcissistic boss, it's essential to find other sources of support and resources to counterbalance the negative effects. Here are some strategies to broaden your network and mitigate the impact of a difficult boss:

1. **Seek Alternative Mentorship:** Look for mentors outside of your current workplace who can offer guidance, support, and career advice. This could include industry professionals, former colleagues, or contacts from professional associations. A mentor from outside your immediate environment can provide a fresh perspective and help you navigate your career development more effectively.

2. **Engage with Professional Communities:** Join professional organizations, attend industry conferences, or participate in networking events related to your field. These activities can help you connect with others in your industry who might offer support, share opportunities, or provide valuable advice.

3. **Develop New Skills:** Invest in your personal and professional growth by enrolling in courses, workshops, or training programs. Gaining new skills or certifications can increase your confidence, open new career opportunities, and reduce your reliance on a difficult boss for professional development.

4. **Build a Support Network:** Establish connections with peers, colleagues, and friends who can offer emotional support and practical advice. Building a supportive network can help you manage stress, gain new perspectives, and maintain a positive outlook despite the challenges posed by your boss.

5. **Explore New Opportunities:** If possible, consider exploring job opportunities within or outside your current organization. Sometimes, finding a new role or workplace can be the best solution for escaping a toxic boss-employee dynamic and advancing your career in a healthier environment.

By broadening your network and seeking support from various sources, you can reduce the impact of a narcissistic boss and foster a more positive and productive professional experience.

B. Structure Your Interaction

When interacting with a narcissistic boss, it's crucial to manage the conversation effectively to avoid unnecessary complications and emotional manipulation. Here's how to structure your interactions:

1. **Keep Interactions Brief and Focused:** Limit the duration of your conversations to avoid giving your boss excessive time to manipulate or dominate the discussion. Aim to be concise and stay on topic. Focus on the specific issues at hand and avoid straying into unrelated areas that could prolong the conversation.

2. **Be Clear and Informative:** Ensure that your communication is direct and fact-based. Present information in a clear, structured manner to minimize the chances of misunderstandings or misinterpretations. Use straightforward language and provide only the necessary details relevant to the topic.

3. **Avoid Emotional Engagement:** Narcissistic bosses may use emotional manipulation to provoke reactions or divert attention. Stay vigilant against such tactics. Keep your responses professional and avoid sharing personal feelings or becoming emotionally involved in the conversation.

4. **Be Firm but Non-Confrontational:** Assertiveness is key when dealing with a narcissistic boss. Clearly state your position and needs without being aggressive. Use confident, calm language and avoid getting drawn into arguments or power struggles. Maintain your boundaries and stand firm on important issues.

5. **Document Interactions:** Whenever possible, keep a record of key communications and decisions made during interactions. This documentation can serve as a reference if disputes arise and helps ensure accountability.

6. **Set Clear Boundaries:** Establish and communicate clear boundaries regarding your availability and limits. For instance, specify your working

hours and be consistent in adhering to them. This helps to manage expectations and reduce opportunities for the boss to exploit or overstep boundaries.

By structuring your interactions in this way, you can maintain professionalism and minimize the impact of a narcissistic boss's behavior on your work and well-being.

C. Avoid Triggers

Narcissists are highly sensitive about their ego and self-esteem, making it crucial to be mindful of behaviors or situations that could provoke a negative reaction. Here's how to navigate interactions with a narcissistic boss effectively:

1. **Identify and Avoid Triggers:** Understand what specific actions or comments might upset or provoke your narcissistic boss. Common triggers include challenges to their authority, criticism, or perceived slights. By identifying these triggers, you can adjust your behavior to avoid unnecessary conflicts.

2. **Be Aware of Their Sensitivity:** Narcissists often react strongly to anything that threatens their self-image or sense of superiority. This includes situations where they feel their status is being undermined or where they perceive a threat to their control. Be cautious about how you frame your feedback or requests to prevent triggering defensive or aggressive responses.

3. **Manage Competitions:** Narcissistic bosses may engage in petty competitions or try to overshadow your achievements to maintain their sense of superiority. If you notice that your boss is taking credit for your work or engaging in competitive behavior, handle it diplomatically. Focus on your contributions and maintain a record of your accomplishments to support your position if needed.

4. **Handle Criticism Carefully:** Narcissists often react poorly to criticism, becoming defensive or hostile when confronted. If you need to provide feedback or address issues, do so in a constructive manner that avoids direct confrontation. Frame your feedback in a way that highlights potential benefits or improvements, rather than focusing solely on their shortcomings.

5. **Appeal to Their Ego:** Leverage their need for admiration and validation by framing requests and interactions in a way that appeals to their sense of importance. For example, if you need advice on a task, present it as an opportunity for them to showcase their expertise and share their valuable experience. Compliment their skills and achievements sincerely, as this can help foster a more positive interaction.

6. **Use Positive Reinforcement:** Narcissists respond well to praise and acknowledgment. When appropriate, offer genuine praise for their contributions or successes. This can help create a more favorable dynamic and reduce the likelihood of conflict.

By carefully managing interactions and avoiding actions that might trigger negative responses, you can maintain a more professional and productive relationship with a narcissistic boss while minimizing unnecessary friction.

D. Engage with Wisdom

Let your interaction always be with wisdom. You can't be wrong while engaging with wisdom.

The Narcissistic Saul and David.

King Saul in the Bible is a classic example of a narcissist. Saul loved the praise of the people. He likes to be in control too even if it means to manipulate. Saul was so proud; he wasn't comfortable with anyone compared to him.

Scenarios of Saul's Narcissistic Behavior

1. After David killed Goliath, the women in the land started singing the praises of David, this didn't go well with Saul. He felt threatened, no one should be praised and admired aside him. So, from that day, he planned to get rid of David.

"And it came to pass as they came, when David was returned from the slaughter of the Philistine, that the women came out of all cities of Israel, singing and dancing, to meet king Saul, with tabrets, with joy, and with instruments of music.

And the women answered one another as they played, and said, Saul hath slain his thousands, and David his ten thousands.

And Saul was very wroth, and the saying displeased him; and he said, they have ascribed unto David ten thousands, and to me they have ascribed but thousands: and what can he have more but the kingdom?

And Saul eyed David from that day and forward.

And Saul cast the javelin; for he said, I will smite David even to the wall with it. And David avoided out of his presence twice"-1Samuel 18: 6-11.

In all of the interaction with Saul, David ensured he acted with wisdom. No wonder he finally got on the throne.

2. Dealing with a Narcissistic Spouse

The dynamics of engaging a narcissist as a spouse are slightly different. Narcissism at home is a terrible thing. It takes joy out of the home and negatively affects the lives of everyone involved.

Ways to Deal with a Narcissistic Spouse

A. Prayer

Prayer can be a source of comfort and strength when dealing with a narcissistic spouse. Many people find solace and guidance through their faith, and it can be a powerful tool for personal resilience and transformation. Here's how prayer can play a role:

1. **Seek Divine Intervention:** Prayer can be a way to ask for divine intervention in your relationship. You may pray for your spouse's heart to be softened and for their behavior to change. Many believe that God has the power to influence people's hearts and minds, and asking for His help can provide a sense of hope and support.

2. **Find Personal Strength:** Use prayer to seek personal strength and wisdom to navigate the challenges of your relationship. Request guidance on how to handle difficult situations and how to maintain your own emotional well-being. Prayer can help you cultivate patience, resilience, and clarity in your interactions.

3. **Foster Compassion and Understanding:** Pray for the ability to view your spouse with compassion and understanding, even in the face of challenging behavior. This perspective can help you manage your responses more effectively and maintain a sense of empathy, which may influence your spouse positively over time.

4. **Pray for Guidance and Insight:** Seek guidance through prayer on how to address issues in your relationship and make decisions that are in your best interest. Request insight into effective strategies for communication and conflict resolution that align with your values and beliefs.

5. **Community and Support:** Consider joining a faith-based support group or seeking counsel from a spiritual advisor. Sharing your struggles with others who have similar beliefs can provide additional support, perspective, and encouragement.

6. **Embrace Hope and Patience:** Understand that change may be gradual, and that prayer is one part of a broader approach to dealing with a

narcissistic spouse. Maintain hope and patience as you navigate your relationship, combining prayer with practical strategies and self-care.

The Bible verse Proverbs 21:1 highlights the belief that "The king's heart is in the hand of the LORD, as the rivers of water: he turneth it whithersoever he will." This verse reinforces the idea that divine influence can play a role in transforming situations and individuals. Through prayer, you can seek support and trust that there is a higher power guiding and supporting you in your journey.

B. Confront Him or Her

Addressing toxic behavior with a narcissistic spouse requires a strategic and composed approach. Here's how to effectively confront your spouse about their behavior:

Prepare Your Points: Before initiating the conversation, clearly identify specific examples of the toxic behavior you want to address. Document instances where their actions or words have negatively impacted you or the relationship. This preparation helps you stay focused and provides concrete evidence to support your concerns.

Choose the Right Time: Find a calm and neutral time to have the conversation, when both you and your spouse are not under stress or engaged in conflict. Avoid discussing these issues during moments of high tension or emotional volatility.

Communicate Firmly but Calmly: Express your concerns in a clear, assertive, but non-confrontational manner. Use "I" statements to convey how their behavior affects you, such as "I feel hurt when you…" or "I am troubled by…" This approach helps to avoid sounding accusatory and reduces the likelihood of triggering defensive reactions.

- **Be Specific and Concrete:** Provide detailed examples of the behavior that is problematic. Instead of generalizing or making vague statements, cite specific incidents and explain why they are troubling. This helps your spouse understand exactly what behavior needs to change.

- **Express Your Feelings and Boundaries:** Clearly state how the toxic behavior is affecting you and your well-being. Let your spouse know that certain behaviors are unacceptable and outline your boundaries. For example, you might say, "I cannot tolerate being spoken to in that manner, and I need you to address me respectfully."

- **Avoid Anger and Blame:** Maintain a calm demeanor throughout the conversation. Refrain from expressing anger or placing blame, as this can escalate the situation and lead to defensiveness. Focus on the impact of their actions rather than attacking their character.

- **Listen and Reflect:** Allow your spouse to respond and listen to their perspective. While this doesn't mean you have to accept their behavior, understanding their viewpoint can help facilitate a more constructive dialogue. Reflect on their responses and consider if there are any underlying issues that need to be addressed.

- **Establish Consequences:** If the toxic behavior continues despite your efforts to address it, be prepared to establish and enforce consequences. This could involve setting limits on your interactions or seeking external support, such as counseling. Make sure the consequences are realistic and clearly communicated.

- **Seek Professional Help:** If addressing the behavior on your own proves challenging, consider involving a therapist or counselor. Professional guidance can provide strategies for managing the relationship dynamics and offer a neutral space for both partners to discuss their issues.

By approaching the confrontation with preparation, clarity, and composure, you can communicate your concerns effectively and encourage a more respectful and healthy interaction with your narcissistic spouse.

C. Seek Out an Authority Figure

If you've addressed the toxic behavior with your narcissistic spouse and they remain unresponsive or unwilling to change, it may be necessary to involve an authority figure who commands their respect. Here's how to approach this step:

Identify a Respected Authority: Determine who in your spouse's life holds significant influence and respect. This could be a trusted mentor, religious leader, respected family member, or a professional advisor. The key is to choose someone who has a genuine impact on your spouse and can speak to them in a way they are likely to listen.

Prepare Your Case: Before approaching the authority figure, gather specific examples of the behavior that has been problematic. Be ready to provide clear, factual details about how this behavior affects you and the relationship. This preparation will help you present a compelling and objective case.

Approach with Sensitivity: When discussing the issue with the authority figure, be respectful and tactful. Explain the situation without exaggerating or making personal attacks. Focus on how the behavior is impacting your relationship and your well-being and seek their guidance on how they might be able to intervene constructively.

Explain the Urgency: Communicate the seriousness of the situation and why it is important for your spouse to address their behavior. Emphasize that the involvement of the authority figure is a last resort after previous attempts to resolve the issue directly have failed.

Request Their Support: Ask the authority figure to provide support in a way that is appropriate for their role. This might include having a private conversation with your spouse, offering counseling or mediation, or providing advice on how to address the behavior. Ensure that their involvement is framed as a supportive measure rather than an adversarial one.

Follow Up: After involving the authority figure, monitor any changes in your spouse's behavior and maintain communication with the authority figure as needed. Provide feedback on the effectiveness of their intervention and discuss any additional support or steps that may be necessary.

Maintain Your Boundaries: Continue to uphold your boundaries and self-care practices, regardless of the outcome of the authority figure's involvement. Their intervention may help, but it's important to remain focused on your own well-being and ensure that your needs are being met.

Evaluate the Relationship: If the involvement of an authority figure does not lead to positive changes and the toxic behavior continues, you may need to reassess the relationship and consider other options, such as seeking professional counseling for yourself or making decisions about the future of the relationship.

By engaging an authority figure who has the respect and influence to address your spouse's behavior, you can potentially facilitate a positive change and seek additional support in managing the dynamics of your relationship.

D. Prioritize Your Well-Being

When dealing with a narcissistic spouse, focusing on your emotional and mental health is crucial. While you hope for positive changes in your spouse, it's essential to take proactive steps to maintain your own well-being. Here's how to prioritize yourself effectively:

1. **Engage in Self-Care:** Make self-care a central part of your routine. Engage in activities that bring you joy and relaxation, such as hobbies, exercise, or spending time with supportive friends. Prioritizing self-care

helps you manage stress and maintain a positive outlook despite the challenges in your relationship.

2. **Find a Support Network:** Seek out a support group or community where you can share your experiences and gain encouragement. Connecting with others who understand your situation can provide valuable emotional support and practical advice. Look for groups related to relationship challenges, mental health, or personal growth.

3. **Pursue Personal Growth:** Invest in your personal development through activities that enhance your skills, knowledge, and self-awareness. Consider pursuing educational opportunities, engaging in creative projects, or participating in self-improvement workshops. Personal growth can boost your confidence and provide a sense of accomplishment.

4. **Set Healthy Boundaries:** Establish and maintain clear boundaries to protect your emotional well-being. This might include limiting the time you spend discussing problematic issues with your spouse or setting boundaries around certain behaviors. Clear boundaries help you manage the impact of your spouse's behavior on your life.

5. **Engage in Spiritual Practices:** If you find solace in your faith, engage in spiritual practices that bring you comfort and strength. This could include prayer, meditation, attending religious services, or reading inspirational texts. Spiritual practices can provide a sense of peace and purpose.

6. **Seek Professional Help:** Consider working with a therapist or counselor to address the emotional impact of living with a narcissistic spouse. Therapy can offer a safe space to explore your feelings, develop coping strategies, and gain insights into managing your relationship dynamics.

7. **Maintain a Balanced Life:** Strive to maintain a balanced life that includes activities and relationships outside of your marriage. Pursue friendships, participate in social activities, and engage in interests that contribute to your overall happiness and well-being.

8. **Monitor Your Mental Health:** Pay attention to your mental and emotional health. Watch for signs of depression or anxiety and seek professional help if needed. Prioritizing mental health is crucial for your overall well-being and can help you navigate the challenges of your relationship more effectively.

9. **Focus on Positivity:** Make a conscious effort to focus on positive aspects of your life. Practice gratitude by acknowledging things you appreciate and enjoy. This positive mindset can help counterbalance the negativity from your relationship and reinforce your resilience.

By prioritizing your well-being and taking active steps to care for yourself, you can better manage the stress and emotional challenges associated with living with a narcissistic spouse. Maintaining your health and happiness is essential for navigating your relationship and ensuring that you remain strong and fulfilled.

CHAPTER 6

Life Jacket

Victims of narcissistic abuse often find themselves starved of genuine love. As human beings, love is a fundamental need—we are wired to give and receive love. When this need goes unmet, it can lead to feelings of worthlessness and low self-esteem. If you've experienced emotional deprivation from a narcissist, you may feel empty, abandoned, or unworthy of love. But in these moments of deprivation, there is a source of love that is boundless, unconditional, and eternal—the love of God.

Understanding God's Love for You

Human love, by nature, is imperfect. It's often transactional, based on the principle of exchange: *I love you, and you love me.* But the reality is that love between people can fluctuate. We may find it difficult to love someone who doesn't love us back, or we may stop loving someone when we feel the love isn't mutual. This is a natural response in human relationships.

However, God's love is different—it is not conditional or based on mutual exchange. God's love does not depend on your love for Him. He loves you even when you feel unlovable, even when you're at your lowest.

The apostle John writes:
"In this was manifested the love of God toward us, because that God sent his only begotten Son into the world, that we might live through him. Herein is love, not that we loved God, but that he loved us, and sent his Son to be the propitiation for our sins."
—1 John 4:9-10

And in Romans, Paul emphasizes:
"For scarcely for a righteous man will one die: yet peradventure for a good man some would even dare

to die. But God commendeth his love toward us, in that, while we were yet sinners, Christ died for us."
—Romans 5:7-8

These verses reveal a powerful truth: God's love is *not* contingent on your actions, your perfection, or your ability to reciprocate. It is unconditional. It is a love so deep that it moved God to send His only Son to die for you—even while you were still far from perfect, even while you were still struggling with your flaws and failures.

The Depth of God's Love for You

God's love for you is not abstract or impersonal; it is deeply intimate and specific. In fact, God's love is so profound that He pays attention to the smallest details of your life. The Bible says that He has numbered the hairs on your head, which is an incredible level of care. Imagine that! The Creator of the universe knows you so intimately, so deeply, that He counts each hair on your head.

This is a love that goes beyond human comprehension. Think about it—no person on earth would take the time to count the hairs on someone's head, but God does. His love is personal, precise, and all-encompassing.

"But the very hairs of your head are all numbered."
—Matthew 10:30

Love is Action: God's Love Demonstrated

God's love isn't just a feeling or a nice idea; it's a tangible, sacrificial action. While human love can sometimes be fleeting or conditional, God's love is steadfast and demonstrated in the most powerful way possible. He didn't just say He loved you; He *showed* it through the sacrifice of Jesus Christ.

"My little children, let us not love in word, neither in tongue; but in deed and in truth."
—1 John 3:18

God didn't just speak His love over you—He acted on it. His love took the form of sending His Son, Jesus, to suffer, die, and rise again so that you could be reconciled to Him, no matter your past mistakes or flaws. God's love is a love of action, a love that reaches into your deepest pain, your most shameful moments, and offers healing, redemption, and unconditional acceptance.

Embracing God's Love for You
Understanding the depth of God's love for you is the key to healing from narcissistic abuse and any emotional wounds that have been inflicted on you. Narcissistic abuse might leave you feeling unworthy, unloved, or forgotten. But God's love is a constant, a source of strength, validation, and healing. He is the Life Jacket that will keep you afloat when you feel like you're drowning in the emotional aftermath of narcissistic manipulation.

When you begin to grasp just how deeply God loves you—when you understand that His love is not based on your performance, but on who you are in Christ—you will start to see yourself differently. You will no longer define your worth based on the opinions or actions of others, but on the eternal, unchanging truth of God's love for you.

A Love Beyond Measure
God's love doesn't just meet you where you are; it lifts you up and transforms you. When you accept God's love, you are no longer at the mercy of people who abuse or manipulate you. You are embraced by a love that knows no limits, no conditions, no end.

Remember, you are *valuable*, not because of anything you've done or failed to do, but because God loves you. You were created in His image, and His love is woven into the very fabric of your being. You don't need to seek love from anyone else to feel worthy—you are already loved beyond measure by the Creator of the universe.

In the face of narcissistic abuse, it is easy to feel invisible, unloved, and unworthy. But God's love is the Life Jacket that will keep you afloat, no matter how rough the waters may seem. You can trust in His perfect love for you, a love that doesn't demand anything from you, but gives everything for you.

Embrace this love. Let it fill the emptiness left by the narcissistic abuse. Let it heal your wounds and renew your self-worth. You are deeply loved by God—never forget that.

Principle of Redemption
To redeem something, you must exchange it for something of equal or greater value. In the case of your redemption, God didn't send an angel or even the highest-ranking archangel to redeem you—because nothing less than the most precious thing could pay the price for your soul. In God's estimation of your worth, only the **precious blood of Jesus** was sufficient. This is a powerful truth to hold on to!

Consider this example: A man once bought a valuable gold chain, intending to sell it later for a profit. A few months later, after an argument with someone, he found that the chain had gone missing. Distraught, he realized he had lost a significant amount of money. A few days later, a neighbor came to him with news—she had found his gold chain. However, she told him he would need to pay a large sum to redeem it. After doing some research into the value of the chain, she decided on an amount that reflected its true worth. The man initially hesitated, reluctant to pay such a high price. But in the end, he realized that it was better to pay the steep cost than to lose the gold chain altogether.

In the same way, when God considered redeeming you, He didn't hold back. He didn't settle for something less valuable. He paid the ultimate price—the **precious blood of His Son**, Jesus Christ. You are worth so much to God, and this is something to be deeply proud of.

Embrace Your Worth in God's Eyes
You might have experienced a relationship, perhaps with a narcissist, that left you feeling unloved, rejected, or unseen. These relationships can leave deep scars, causing you to doubt your value. You may have felt that no one truly cared for you, or that you weren't worthy of love. But let this truth sink in: **God loves you deeply**, beyond the capacity of any human being to love you.

The love that God has for you is immeasurable, perfect, and unchanging. In the face of negative experiences, toxic relationships, or painful circumstances, you must anchor yourself in this unshakable truth: **You are loved by God**—the Creator of the universe. You are not alone. You are not abandoned. No matter what others may have made you feel, God's love for you is eternal and unbreakable.

The Price of Your Redemption
When God chose to redeem you, He didn't spare any cost. The price He paid was **the life of His Son**, the most precious thing He had. That's how much He values you. It's easy to feel worthless when you've been mistreated or manipulated, but God sees you as priceless. His love for you is far beyond any human love. It is not based on what you can offer or how you've behaved. It is not influenced by your past mistakes or your shortcomings. You are loved because **you are His creation**, and He sees immeasurable value in you.

So, whenever you feel dejected, rejected, or unloved by others, remember that God's love for you far exceeds what anyone on earth can offer. You are worth more than you can imagine, and nothing can change how He feels about you.

God redeemed you with the precious blood of Jesus—this is the ultimate demonstration of His love for you. You are of great worth in His sight, and nothing will ever diminish the value He places on you. In times of pain, rejection, or self-doubt, hold fast to this truth: **You are loved deeply by God**. Embrace that love, rest in it, and let it transform the way you see yourself.

Loving Yourself
When you don't love yourself, it becomes difficult—if not impossible—to fully receive love from others. The love and affection others offer may never feel like enough because the deep, internal need for **self-love** remains unmet. No external love can fill the void that only **self-acceptance** and **self-worth** can fill.

In addition, when you fail to love yourself, you are also limited in your ability to love others. You can't pour from an empty cup. True love is an overflow of the love you have for yourself. When you are at peace with who you are, it becomes natural to extend love to others in a healthy, authentic way.

This is a critical issue for narcissists. At their core, narcissists struggle with a lack of self-love and self-acceptance. They have no internal peace or sense of worth, which leads them to compensate in unhealthy ways. To cover up their own insecurities, they manipulate, belittle, and mistreat others. Their inability to love themselves is at the root of their toxic behavior toward others. When you don't know how to love yourself, it becomes almost impossible to love others in a genuine, meaningful way.

Things that Hinder Self-love

A. Wrong association

B. Guilt

C. Ingratitude

A. Wrong Association

The people you associate with can have a significant impact on your self-love. Healthy, positive relationships should support your sense of self-worth and respect, but toxic relationships can erode it. If you're constantly surrounded by people who belittle or criticize you, it will be difficult to see your own value.

A toxic relationship, whether with a friend, a family member, or a partner, often revolves around negative comments, body-shaming, or outright disrespect. Over time, these interactions can make you feel inadequate, unworthy, and undeserving of love. You might even start to internalize their negative views about you.

On the other hand, healthy relationships are built on mutual love, honor, and respect. When you are in an environment where your value is affirmed and nurtured, it becomes easier to love yourself. But when you surround yourself with people who constantly put you down, you open yourself up to manipulation, especially by narcissists. Narcissists prey on those who lack self-love and self-worth because they know they can control and manipulate them. Never allow yourself to be in such relationships—your value is far greater than that.

B. Guilt from the Past

Guilt is one of the most debilitating emotions you can experience, especially when it keeps you tethered to the past. It prevents you from moving forward and can even block your ability to heal. Those who are plagued by guilt often find it hard to see the good in their present lives because they are fixated on past mistakes or decisions. This makes it nearly impossible to embrace self-love, as guilt keeps you trapped in a cycle of self-condemnation.

Satan often uses guilt as a weapon to sabotage your growth and prevent you from experiencing the peace and freedom God offers. The more you focus on your past failures, the more you distance yourself from God's grace and forgiveness. Guilt clouds your mind, making it difficult to move forward or enjoy the blessings of today. It tells you that you are unworthy of love, forgiveness, and success—none of which is true.

But here's the truth: **Guilt is a lie.** Jesus already paid the price for your sins, mistakes, and failures. The enemy wants to keep you in a place of condemnation, but God wants you to walk in freedom and forgiveness.

Antidote to Guilt: Understanding What Jesus Did for You

The only way to break free from guilt is to understand what Jesus did on your behalf. Satan thrives in ignorance, which is why the Bible says, "My people perish for lack of knowledge" (Hosea 4:6). When you know the truth of what Christ has done for you, it will set you free from the chains of guilt.

Jesus became the ultimate **scapegoat** for your sins. In the Old Testament, on the Day of Atonement, the high priest would lay his hands on a goat and confess the sins of the people, then send the goat into the wilderness, symbolically carrying the sins away (Leviticus 16:21-22). This act foreshadowed

Jesus, who took all of your sins upon Himself and carried them away to be remembered no more.

The Bible says, "For He [God] made Him [Jesus] who knew no sin to be sin for us, that we might become the righteousness of God in Him" (2 Corinthians 5:21). This means that when Jesus died on the cross, He took your guilt, shame, and condemnation upon Himself. You are now justified—meaning that you are legally declared "not guilty" before God.

So, when guilt tries to overwhelm you, remember that Jesus has already paid for your sins, and you are forgiven. If you've confessed your sins and turned to God, then there's no room for guilt. Guilt doesn't have the right to keep you in bondage. You are free.

C. Ingratitude

Another barrier to self-love is ingratitude. When you focus on what you don't have or the mistakes you've made, it becomes easy to lose sight of the many blessings and positive aspects of your life. Ingratitude breeds a sense of lack and dissatisfaction, preventing you from fully appreciating who you are and what you've accomplished.

Gratitude, on the other hand, helps you focus on the good. When you cultivate a heart of thankfulness, you start to recognize your worth and the many things that make you valuable. Gratitude shifts your focus from what's wrong with your life to what's right, and it opens your heart to receive God's love and the love of others.

The key to overcoming ingratitude is to actively practice thankfulness. Take time each day to reflect on the things you're grateful for. Even in the midst of pain and struggle, there is always something to be thankful for. Gratitude allows you to see the value in yourself and your life, regardless of the challenges you may face.

Drawing Strength from God

When life's difficulties seem overwhelming, and you feel like you can't go on, it's easy to give up. But God promises to renew your strength when you seek Him. Isaiah 40:29-31 assures us that "He gives power to the faint, and to those who have no might, He increases strength." When you feel weak, it's a sign that you need to rely on God's strength, which is made perfect in your weakness (2 Corinthians 12:9).

Sometimes, the crises you face will drain every ounce of energy from you, and you may feel like quitting. But in those moments, God is right there to offer you the strength you need to keep going. You don't have to rely on your own strength—God is your refuge and your strength (Psalm 46:1).

Learning to Talk to God
One of the most beautiful ways to draw strength from God is through prayer. Prayer is a personal conversation with God—an exchange where you pour out your heart and receive His strength in return. Talking to God doesn't need to be formal or religious. Simply speak from your heart, share your pain, fears, and hopes, and He will meet you in that place of vulnerability.

Prayer is a structure of exchange: you give God your hurt, and He gives you peace. You share your struggles, and He provides the strength to persevere. "Cast all your cares upon Him, for He cares for you" (1 Peter 5:7). When you bring your burdens to God in prayer, He will comfort you and help you move forward with renewed strength.

God isn't just interested in your spiritual well-being—He cares deeply about every area of your life. Whether you're dealing with pain from the past or challenges in the present, He is always ready to listen and give you the strength to move forward.

God's Love Is Your Advantage
The comfort God provides is uniquely personal. He meets you exactly where you are, understanding the depth of your pain in a way no one else can. His

love is designed to heal, restore, and strengthen you. When you turn to Him, you can be confident that His love is sufficient to carry you through even the hardest seasons of life.

In those moments when your heart feels heavy and the weight of life's challenges seems too much to bear, remember that you are loved beyond measure. God is with you, and His love is the anchor that will keep you steady through the storm.

Self-love is not just about accepting yourself—it's about acknowledging your worth in God's eyes, understanding His forgiveness, and drawing strength from His love and comfort. As you work through the obstacles that hinder self-love—wrong associations, guilt, and ingratitude—you'll begin to see yourself the way God sees you: valuable, loved, and worthy of His grace.

CHAPTER 7

The Beauty of Your Scars — Turning Your Pain Into Gain

Anyone who has experienced the deep emotional wounds caused by narcissistic abuse understands how it can bring your life to a screeching halt. The pain is so intense that, without proper healing, it can be overwhelming. Many victims of narcissistic abuse find themselves spiraling into depression, while some even contemplate suicide. The journey to healing and reclaiming your life requires immense effort, support, and determination. But despite how difficult it may seem, it is possible to rise from the ashes of this trauma and emerge stronger, wiser, and more whole than before.

The emotional pain caused by narcissism cuts deep because it doesn't just affect the surface; it affects the very core of your being—the soul. The soul encompasses your emotions, will, and reasoning, all of which are the essence of who you are as a person. When these are wounded, you may lose the will to live, or your emotions may become numb, leaving you unable to feel joy, passion, or enthusiasm for life. This loss of drive and emotional apathy is what leads many victims of narcissistic abuse to experience depression and suicidal thoughts.

In addition to crippling the will and emotions, narcissistic abuse can distort your thinking. It can make you question your reality, cause you to doubt your worth, and even convince you that you're undeserving of love or happiness. The damage to your mind can be just as profound as the damage to your heart. But even in the darkest of places, there is hope. You **can** heal from the trauma inflicted by narcissism and move toward a brighter, more fulfilled life.

Saving Your Soul; Healing Your Mind

The path to healing begins with the transformation of your mind and soul. As difficult as it may seem, the first step toward recovery is to open yourself up to light—the light of God's word. The Bible speaks of this transformative power:

James 1:21:
"Therefore, lay aside all filthiness and overflow of wickedness, and receive with meekness the implanted word, which is able to save your souls."

This verse highlights that the word of God is powerful enough to heal and restore your soul. It is a balm for every wound caused by narcissism. It is not just spiritual advice—it's a profound, healing force that has the power to reach the deepest parts of you and begin the work of restoration.

Proverbs 4:20-22 further reinforces this:
"My son, give attention to my words; incline your ear to my sayings. Do not let them depart from your eyes; keep them in the midst of your heart; For they are life to those who find them, and health to all their flesh."

When you open yourself to God's word, it begins to infiltrate your mind and soul. It works like a spiritual medicine, healing and restoring what has been broken. Over time, you'll notice a shift in your inner world. Where there was once sadness, there will be joy; where there was once despair, there will be hope. The more you immerse yourself in God's truth, the more strength you'll gain to face life's challenges.

Healing from narcissistic trauma isn't instant. It's a process. But as you continue to let the word of God saturate your heart and mind, you'll begin to feel the effects. The depressive thoughts that once held you captive will start to lose their power. Your emotions will begin to realign with the truth of who you are—valuable, worthy of love, and capable of experiencing joy again.

Turning Your Pain into Gain

Your scars, while painful reminders of the past, are not the end of your story. In fact, they are a testimony to your survival and strength. **The beauty of your scars** lies in the resilience and wisdom it represents. No, the pain was not easy, but it has forged something new in you—an ability to overcome, to heal, and to grow.

One of the most powerful aspects of healing from narcissistic abuse is the ability to transform your pain into something positive. Your story of survival can inspire others who are still in the dark, struggling to make sense of their own pain. Your scars become symbols of hope—proof that it is possible to emerge from the ashes of trauma and rebuild a life that is even more beautiful than before.

As you heal, you may find that your past pain becomes a source of compassion for others who are going through similar struggles. Your ability to empathize with those suffering from emotional wounds will deepen, and your capacity for love and understanding will grow. You can use the lessons you've learned through your pain to help others find their way out of the darkness.

The Power of Transformation

The healing process can be compared to a butterfly emerging from its cocoon. The struggle the butterfly faces in breaking free from its shell makes it stronger, and it is through this process that it is transformed into something far more beautiful than it was before. Similarly, the challenges you've faced, painful as they were, have the potential to transform you into someone more resilient, compassionate, and wise.

In the same way that God can take your brokenness and turn it into beauty, He can also use your scars to impact others. **You are not defined by your pain**—you are defined by how you respond to it. The journey of healing is one of personal growth and empowerment, and it is a process that will make you more whole than you ever were before.

Embracing Your New Identity

As you continue to heal, remember that your true identity is not tied to the abuse you endured. You are not defined by what was done to you, but by who you are in Christ. Your scars are part of your story, but they do not determine your future. The future God has for you is full of hope, peace, and purpose.

You are not the sum of your pain—you are the sum of God's love, grace, and redemption. Embrace this new identity. Stand tall in the truth that you are more than a survivor; you are a conqueror, empowered to live a life full of purpose and joy. And as you walk in this newfound strength, remember that your scars are beautiful—they are a testament to the incredible journey you've been through and the even more incredible future ahead of you.

Healing from narcissistic abuse is a long, sometimes painful process, but it is also a journey of transformation. The scars left by narcissism do not have to define you—they can serve as reminders of how far you've come and the strength you've gained. Through God's word, His love, and His healing power, you can turn your pain into something beautiful. You are not just a victim of narcissistic abuse; you are a survivor, and with God's help, you will rise to become the best version of yourself.

Benefits of Receiving the Word into Your Soul

1. Comfort of the Spirit

When you immerse yourself in God's Word, He brings comfort to the areas where you need it most. Comfort is God's way of helping you to endure and overcome the difficulties you're facing without breaking under the pressure.

Psalm 71:21:
"Thou shalt increase my greatness, and comfort me on every side."

This comfort manifests as a peace that surpasses understanding—an unexplainable peace that stands in stark contrast to your circumstances. Even amidst turmoil, there is a quiet assurance, a peace that you can't trace to any source other than God Himself. This peace is not dependent on the external situation; it is a supernatural gift that only the Lord can give. The Word of God is the vehicle that ushers in this peace, reminding you that God is in control and is working all things for your good. This peace is the first step in your healing process, a signal that God is working in your heart and soul to restore what was broken.

2. **Strength in Time of Need**

   God supplies His strength to us through His Word, providing an inner strength that enables us to endure and thrive even when we feel weak and exhausted. This strength is not just physical; it is a spiritual fortitude that helps you stand firm when everything else seems to be falling apart.

Isaiah 40:29-31:

"He giveth power to the faint; and to them that have no might he increaseth strength. Even the youths shall faint and be weary, and the young men shall utterly fall: But they that wait upon the LORD shall renew their strength; they shall mount up with wings as eagles; they shall run, and not be weary; and they shall walk, and not faint."

When emotional trauma takes its toll, you can't rely on your own strength. The Word of God provides the reinforcement you need to keep going. Even the strongest among us, symbolized by the "youths" in this passage, will falter in the face of overwhelming trials. Only those who draw their strength from God will be able to stand firm. This is why we must lean on Him for support—His strength will never fail.

3. **Joy**

   The Word of God is a source of true, lasting joy. This is especially vital for those who have been wounded by narcissistic abuse, as such trauma often strips away any semblance of happiness. But God's Word replenishes you with something greater than fleeting happiness—it restores you with the joy of the Lord.

Joy is far superior to happiness. While happiness is dependent on external circumstances, joy transcends all situations. It is an internal strength that can sustain you through any trial. The joy that comes from God is always active, independent of your circumstances, and it has the power to heal the negative emotions often experienced by victims of narcissistic abuse.

When you are filled with God's joy, it drives out bitterness and negativity. It lifts your eyes off the offenses and disappointments that once held you captive, and it renews your drive and enthusiasm for life. With joy in your heart, you begin to find pleasure in things again, and your perspective on life shifts from sorrow to hope.

4. Direction

One of the most common struggles for victims of narcissistic abuse is confusion—uncertainty about what to do, where to go, and what the future holds. God's Word offers clear guidance, helping you find the direction you need to move forward in your life.

As human beings, our understanding is limited. We cannot see the end from the beginning, and often, we make decisions based on partial information, which can lead us astray.

Proverbs 14:12:
"There is a way that seems right to a man, but its end is the way of death."

This verse highlights the fact that our human judgment is flawed. We might think we know what's best, but only God knows the true outcome of every choice. This is why we are encouraged to lean on Him, the One who knows the end from the beginning.

God, in His infinite wisdom, knows what is best for us at every moment. When we spend time in His Word, He sheds light on our path and provides us with clear direction. His guidance is always in our best interest, leading us to a future filled with hope and peace.

Proverbs 3:5-6:
"Trust in the LORD with all your heart, and lean not on your own understanding. In all your ways acknowledge Him, and He shall direct your paths."

Spending time in God's Word opens our hearts to His guidance. As we surrender our understanding to Him, He directs our steps, ensuring that we make choices that align with His perfect plan for our lives.

The Word of God is a powerful tool that can bring healing, strength, joy, and direction into your life. By receiving God's Word into your soul, you open yourself to the comfort of the Spirit, the strength you need in times of weakness, the joy that transcends circumstances, and the direction that leads you toward God's perfect will. No matter what you've been through, God's Word is the key to restoring your soul and giving you the tools you need to move forward with confidence and peace.

Chapter 8

Owning Your Life

Relating to a narcissist often leaves deep emotional scars. Victims of narcissistic abuse may experience a wide range of negative effects, from depression and low self-esteem to anxiety and a general lack of enthusiasm for life. These wounds can make it difficult to move forward, but healing begins when you realize one important truth: **you own your life**. The power to shape your future and move beyond the pain is in your hands.

Narcissists thrive on dominating others, manipulating their thoughts and actions. But it doesn't have to be this way. **You do not have to allow anyone to control your life**. God has entrusted you with the power to make decisions about your own journey, and you are not beholden to anyone's toxic influence.

It's time to stop living as though your life is at the mercy of others. This kind of mindset opens the door for manipulation and control, especially by someone like a narcissist. Once you realize that **you are the steward of your life**, you will regain the strength to move forward, no matter how tough it may seem.

Reclaiming Your Power

Yes, healing from narcissistic abuse is difficult. The hurt runs deep, and there may be times when you feel lost or unsure of what to do next. But **God's plan for your life is greater than any pain you've experienced**. His purpose for you goes beyond the trauma of the past, and His commitment to your future is unshakeable.

The truth is the enemy will try to overwhelm you with negative emotions—sadness, despair, and thoughts that you are powerless. He will bring up the memories of your abuse to keep you stuck in the past, distracted from the future that God is calling you to. **Do not let these negative feelings dictate your reality.**

It's normal to feel the weight of your past experiences, especially in the aftermath of narcissistic abuse. But you must **resist the pull** of those emotions that seek to drag you back into hopelessness. The enemy's goal is to keep you trapped in defeat, as though there is no way forward. He wants you to remain stuck in a place of emotional slavery, just as the Israelites were in Egypt, unable to envision the freedom of the promised land.

The Power of Your Response

In those moments when negative emotions rise within you—when the weight of your circumstances feels too much to bear—remember this: **you have the power to choose your response**. The enemy wants you to give in, to believe that the pain is insurmountable, and that you are stuck forever. But **you don't have to let these feelings control you**.

Giving in to despair or self-doubt will only expose you to the manipulation of the enemy. He is a master of deception, and he will use every emotion you experience as a weapon against you. When you give in to sadness, resentment, or fear, you open yourself to the enemy's tactics. But when you stand firm in the truth that **God has a plan for you**—a plan filled with hope, healing, and purpose—you will begin to reclaim your power and break free from the past.

The enemy's ultimate goal is to wear you down, to make you feel defeated and unworthy of God's promises. He wants you to remain in emotional bondage, unwilling to take the courageous steps toward freedom. But God is calling you to rise up, just as He called the Israelites to leave Egypt and enter the promised land.

Moving Forward
The road to healing may not be easy, but it is possible. **Take ownership of your life**. Refuse to let anyone, especially the enemy, dictate how you feel or

what you believe about yourself. Embrace the truth that **God's plan for you is greater than any hurt or setback you've faced.**

In those moments of struggle, when you feel overwhelmed by sadness or confusion, take a deep breath and remind yourself: **I own my life. I have the power to choose how I move forward. I am not a victim—I am a victor in Christ.**

Your past does not define you. Your future, in God's hands, is filled with hope, purpose, and healing. Trust in His promises and take the courageous steps toward reclaiming your life.

Own Your Joy!

When someone has experienced narcissistic abuse, their self-image and sense of worth can be severely distorted. Often, the result is a pessimistic view of oneself and life in general. The pain from the abuse may cause you to see the world through a lens of negativity, making it difficult to envision any positive outcomes. Yet, **the mindset you choose to adopt will shape your reality**.

A person who consistently holds a negative, pessimistic view of life will find it almost impossible to achieve anything meaningful or fulfilling. Such a mindset can keep you stuck in a cycle of mediocrity and unfulfillment—far from the life you were meant to live. While it's understandable to feel down after enduring emotional trauma, **staying in that place is a choice**—and it's a choice that leads to further harm.

The Joy Therapy

One of the most powerful tools you can use to combat a pessimistic mindset is **joy therapy**. Joy therapy is a deliberate, conscious choice to embrace joy at all times, regardless of how you feel in the moment. It means **replacing negative emotions with joy**—choosing joy as a form of inner strength, no matter the circumstances.

A person who can control their emotions and choose their response to life's challenges is a person who is truly empowered. **This is the kind of power you need to reclaim your life from narcissistic abuse.** If you allow your emotions to dictate your actions, you risk being manipulated by others, particularly by narcissists who use your emotions against you.

Choosing joy is one of the most effective ways to regain control over your life. **It's not always easy**—especially in the beginning. There will be days when joy seems impossible to summon. But remember, **joy is not a fleeting emotion based on external circumstances**. It is a choice, a mindset, and a practice that you can cultivate, regardless of the external world around you.

Joy Beyond Circumstances
Throughout our lives, we've been conditioned to find joy only in certain circumstances: when we receive a compliment, get a promotion, or experience something exciting. Happiness, in these cases, is often contingent on something external. But **joy therapy** works differently. In this practice, your joy is **not dependent on anything outside of you**. It is an internal decision that you make to hold joy as your default setting—regardless of what's happening around you.

For example, when someone fails to notice your achievements or offer a compliment, you may feel discouraged or overlooked. But with joy therapy, **you choose joy even in those moments.** Your joy is no longer tied to external validation. It is a resolute stance you take in life. **This kind of joy shields you from external negativity and makes you resilient against narcissistic manipulation.**

While you may not be able to control what others do or the pain that comes from abuse, **you can control your response to it.** By choosing joy, you protect yourself from further emotional harm. You take back the power that was once stolen from you, and you shift the narrative from victimhood to empowerment.

How to Cultivate Joy

Joy is an internal resource, one that must be sustained by something greater than external circumstances. **The key to lasting joy is an awareness of God's plan for your life.** When you understand that God's intentions for you are good and that He has a beautiful future in store for you, joy becomes sustainable—even in the hardest of times.

As Jeremiah 29:11 says:

"I know the plans I have for you," declares the Lord, "plans to prosper you and not to harm you, plans to give you a hope and a future." (Jeremiah 29:11, NIV)

This kind of assurance is the bedrock of unshakable joy. Knowing that **God's plans for you are secure**—and that they remain unaffected by the hurt others have caused you—gives you the confidence to rejoice no matter the circumstances. The pain of the past cannot stop God's good plan for your future. In fact, **God uses the very things people meant to harm you as the raw material for something greater in your life.** His power is so great that He can turn even the worst experiences into a steppingstone for your growth and healing.

This truth is what sustains joy: **the certainty that no one, and nothing, can thwart God's purpose for your life.** Knowing that **all things work together for your good** (Romans 8:28) allows you to rest in joy, trusting that God is using every moment—even the painful ones—for your benefit.

Re-evaluation: Turning Pain into Purpose

Healing from narcissistic abuse involves more than just letting go of pain; it also requires reflection and **personal growth.** Take time to evaluate your life and the choices that have led you here—not from a place of regret, but from a desire to grow and become wiser.

Ask yourself: *What could I have done differently that might have shielded me from narcissistic abuse? What decisions or patterns in my life made me vulnerable to manipulation?* This isn't about blaming yourself, but about gaining wisdom so that you can make healthier choices moving forward. **This reflection will help you take responsibility for your life and empower you to create a future that aligns with your highest good.**

Choosing Your Joy
Remember, joy is a decision. It is a practice, a mindset, and a stance you take in your life. **No one can take away your joy unless you give it up.** As you embrace joy therapy, you are choosing to reclaim your happiness and power, no matter what has happened to you in the past. With joy as your foundation, you will begin to see the world differently—and with God's plan for you firmly in mind, you'll step into the future with confidence, peace, and resilience.

CHAPTER 9

Company of the Strong: Finding the Right Support Group

"Two are better than one... If either of them falls down, one can help the other up. But pity anyone who falls and has no one to help them up." — Ecclesiastes 4:9-10

Healing from narcissistic abuse is a journey that should never be walked alone. **Everyone needs a support system**—a community of people who cheer you on, encourage you, and help you keep moving forward. In the aftermath of narcissistic abuse, it's crucial to distance yourself from those who bring you down or make you question your worth. Narcissists are skilled at distorting your self-image, making you feel inferior or unworthy. But **God sees you as a unique, valuable creation**, not a lesser being. You deserve to surround yourself with people who see you for who you truly are and who will help you rebuild your self-esteem and confidence.

The company of positive, uplifting individuals can be a powerful source of healing. Whether it's a friend, a spouse, a family member, or a mentor, you need people who will **help you rise from the ashes of depression and low self-worth**. These are the people who will speak life into you, pray for you, and help you see a brighter future.

The Struggle to Trust Again

After the deep betrayal of narcissistic abuse, it's understandable if you find it difficult to trust others. Narcissistic abuse often leaves scars that make it hard to open up to anyone else. You might fear being hurt again or feel vulnerable and exposed. But it's important to remember that **not everyone is like the** narcissist you've encountered. There are people who have walked similar paths, come out stronger, and are ready to offer support. **These are the people you need to seek out.**

Surrounding yourself with a supportive, positive community is essential for your healing and growth. **Being around people who are strong in faith, who believe in your future, and who want to see you succeed** will help you face the challenges ahead with courage. They will encourage you when you feel down and remind you of your strength when you forget it.

Opening Yourself to Help

The first step in finding the right support is **being open to receiving help.** It can be difficult to admit that you need others, especially after being manipulated and hurt by a narcissist. But acknowledging that you need support is not a sign of weakness—it's a step toward strength. It's a sign that you are ready to heal, to move forward, and to open yourself to new possibilities. Once you admit to yourself that you need help, you will be much closer to finding it.

Steps to Finding the Right Company

1. **Reflect on the People Around You**
   Take a close look at your current relationships. Are there people who consistently bring you down or make you feel smaller than you are? Narcissistic individuals often surround themselves with people they can control, and their toxic influence can be subtle but harmful. **Identify who truly uplifts you, listens without judgment, and genuinely cares for your well-being.** These are the people who belong in your inner circle.

2. **Seek Out Like-Minded Individuals**
   Look for people who have walked through similar struggles and emerged stronger. Whether it's through support groups, therapy, or online communities, **finding others who have shared experiences can help**

you feel understood and supported. **Being around people who have healed from narcissistic** abuse will give you the courage to keep moving forward.

3. **Be Intentional About Boundaries**
   While it's important to seek support, it's equally important to set boundaries with those who are negative or toxic. Protect your emotional well-being by saying **"no"** to people who drain you or bring unnecessary drama into your life. Your healing is your priority, and **protecting your peace** should always come first.

4. **Allow Yourself to Be Vulnerable**
   Opening up to others can be difficult, especially if you've been hurt before. But true healing requires vulnerability. **The right people will not use your vulnerabilities against you**; instead, they will offer support, understanding, and encouragement. Allowing yourself to be vulnerable is not a weakness—**it's a sign of strength**. It shows you trust yourself to heal, and that you are open to growing and learning with others.

5. **Invest in Relationships That Support Your Growth**
   Once you find the right people, invest in those relationships. Share your dreams, struggles, and goals with them. Let them help you stay accountable to your healing journey. **Healthy, supportive relationships not only help you recover** from narcissistic abuse but also help you grow into a stronger, more resilient version of yourself.

The Power of the Right Company

The company you keep can either **lift you up or drag you down**. After narcissistic abuse, it's essential to surround yourself with people who are strong, encouraging, and uplifting. These individuals will help you rebuild your confidence, face your fears, and move forward with a renewed sense of purpose.

Remember, **healing is a team effort**. No one heals in isolation. By opening yourself up to the right support group, you give yourself the chance to **thrive** again. You are not meant to carry the weight of the world alone—God designed us for connection, and through the right community, you will find strength, healing, and joy.

Additional Key Steps for Finding the Right Support

1. **Detach from Narcissists**

    It's easy to recognize when you find yourself in the midst of narcissistic individuals—they often display a superiority complex, a condescending attitude, and a tendency to control others. **Being in the company of such people hinders your progress** by keeping you depressed, frustrated, and unsure of your worth. Detach yourself from them for the sake of your healing. Distance is crucial to living a better, healthier life. ·

2. **Position Yourself for the Right People**

    Finding the right people requires **open-mindedness**. Just because you've encountered narcissists before doesn't mean you can't find healthy, supportive people now. **Be open to meeting new people** and allow yourself to gradually accept others into your life. Pray that God will bring the right people into your path—**God answers prayers,** and He knows exactly who can help you in your healing process. **Reach out to people who have overcome similar struggles**, as they have the wisdom to guide you through your recovery. **Don't shut yourself off to potential healing relationships**. Take small steps towards connecting with others who can encourage you.

3. **Learn to Trust Again**

    Trust is the belief in the character and ability of another person. After being betrayed, learning to trust again can be challenging, but it is vital for your recovery. **Ensure that the people you trust have proven themselves trustworthy.** Trusting others may take time, but it's essential for your healing process. **The right people can only help you if you allow them** to do so. Trust them and be open to their guidance. **The healing process accelerates when you are open to trusting the right people.**

Being in the right company cannot be overemphasized. It is essential for your recovery from narcissistic abuse. When you surround yourself with strong, encouraging people, you gain the strength to heal and grow. Walking with wise and supportive individuals helps you recover and emerge stronger than before. As the Scriptures say, "Walk with the wise and you will become wise." In the same way, walking with strong people helps you grow stronger.

As you look back on your journey, you will be able to see the progress you've made. You will have a lot to be thankful for, as you witness the restoration of your life and experience healing from the abuse. Keep walking with the strong—soon, you will find yourself strong as well.

CHAPTER 10

Memoir: Lessons from My Memory Lane

I've often felt a deep, undeniable calling from God to share my journey—not just as a story, but as a living testimony of His healing power. The experiences I write about are not theoretical or abstract ideas; they are the real, raw emotions and struggles that I've faced. **I write from a place of personal experience**, from a heart that has known the depths of pain and the power of restoration. My journey has been one of healing, and through it all, I have learned that no matter how deep the wound, **God's grace can reach deeper**.

As I reflect on the chapters of my life, I see how God has taken me through seasons of intense hurt, struggle, and confusion. Yet, with each step, He has shown me that there is purpose in the pain. **The wounds of the past have not only been healed**, but they have been transformed into lessons, wisdom, and hope for others who may be walking a similar path.

One of the most profound and painful seasons of my life was when I found myself in the grips of **narcissistic abuse**. If you've ever been in the clutches of such manipulation, you know it's more than just emotional pain—it's a deep, soul-crushing experience that distorts your sense of self and makes you question everything you thought you knew about love, trust, and even your own worth.

It's a time I would never wish to revisit. There were days I wondered if I would ever recover, if I would ever feel whole again. But through God's grace, I was not only able to **survive** but to thrive. I look back now, not with bitterness, but with deep gratitude for the lessons learned. **The struggles of that time were the very things that shaped the person I am today**—stronger, wiser, and more compassionate.

I am sharing these lessons with you because I know what it feels like to be trapped in a cycle of self-doubt, confusion, and emotional turmoil. **I know what it's like to feel lost**, to wonder if you'll ever see the light at the end of the tunnel. But I also know the hope that comes from knowing that **you are not alone**, that healing is possible, and that you are worthy of the peace and joy that God has waiting for you.

Here are some of the key lessons I've learned through my journey of healing from narcissistic abuse—lessons that I believe can speak directly to your heart, no matter where you find yourself in your own healing process.

Lesson 1: You Are Not What They Say You Are
When you're in a relationship with a narcissist, they will try to convince you that you are less than you are—that you are not enough, not worthy of love, not deserving of respect. Narcissists have a way of making you feel small and insignificant, of chipping away at your self-esteem until you question your own worth.

But I want to remind you of something incredibly important: **You are not what they say you are.** You are a beloved child of God, created in His image and filled with inherent worth. No one, no matter how convincing or manipulative, has the right to define your value. **God sees you differently**—He sees you as precious, strong, and capable of amazing things. It took me a long time to truly believe this, but when I did, it was like a veil was lifted from my eyes.

Lesson 2: Healing Takes Time, and That's Okay
When I first started my healing journey, I wanted it to be quick. I wanted to snap my fingers and be "healed," but that's not how it works. Healing takes time, and it's okay to feel frustrated by the pace. **Some days will be better than others**, and that's normal. **There's no set timeline for healing**—it's a process, and there will be setbacks along the way. But don't be discouraged. **The fact that you're moving forward, even in small steps, is progress.**

I had to learn to be patient with myself. I had to stop trying to rush my healing or berate myself for not being "over it" fast enough. **It's okay to take the time you need** to heal and find peace. Healing doesn't happen in a straight line—it's often messy and unpredictable. But it is happening, and with each day, you are getting closer to the person God has destined you to be.

Lesson 3: You Have the Power to Reclaim Your Life

When you're in an abusive relationship, especially with a narcissist, it often feels like you have no control. You feel trapped, like your life is no longer your own. The narcissist controls the narrative, the emotions, the actions, and often your sense of self. I know the feeling of being powerless—of feeling like I had no say in my own life.

But **one of the most empowering lessons I've learned is this**: You have the power to reclaim your life. It may not feel like it at first, but **you have the power to make choices, to set boundaries, to take back control** over your emotions, your environment, and your future. It's a long process, but as you begin to reclaim those pieces of yourself that were lost or stolen, you'll find your strength again.

One of the biggest turning points in my journey came when I finally realized that **I didn't need anyone's permission to heal**. I didn't need to stay trapped in a cycle of abuse or self-doubt. **I could choose to move forward.** That realization was life changing.

Lesson 4: Your Past Does Not Define Your Future

There were times when I couldn't see beyond the pain. The wounds were so deep, and the scars seemed so permanent that I thought they would always be a part of me. I thought my past would forever define who I was. But one of the most beautiful truths I've learned is that **your past does not have to define your future**.

The abuse you've endured does not determine your worth, and it certainly does not determine the direction your life will take. **God has a new plan for you**—one of healing, growth, and purpose. I've come to realize that **God uses**

even the darkest moments of our lives to bring about transformation. What I thought would break me has, in fact, been the very thing that has propelled me into a better, stronger version of myself.

You may not see it right now, but **your future holds so much more than you can imagine**. Trust that God has a plan for you, and that plan is good.

Lesson 5: Forgiveness is Freedom
This lesson was the hardest one for me. I wanted to hold onto my pain and anger because it felt like the only thing that kept me safe. But what I didn't realize was that **holding onto that bitterness was only holding me back**. It wasn't hurting the narcissist—it was hurting me.

Forgiveness doesn't mean excusing the hurt or pretending it didn't happen. It doesn't mean forgetting the abuse. Forgiveness is about releasing yourself from the chains of resentment and anger. **Forgiveness is not for them; it's for you.** It's a step toward freedom—freedom from the past, freedom from the power the abuser holds over you, and freedom to live the life God has called you to live.

When I finally let go of the anger, I found peace. **True peace comes when we release others into God's hands**, trusting that He will take care of the justice and vengeance. **Forgiving doesn't mean you have to stay in toxic relationships**, it means you are no longer controlled by the hurt.

Lesson 6: You Are Not Alone
Finally, perhaps the most important lesson I've learned is this: **You are not alone**. If you are walking through the pain of narcissistic abuse right now, it can feel incredibly isolating. It can feel like no one understands the depth of what you're going through. But I'm here to tell you that there are others who have walked this path, who have been where you are, and who are proof that healing is possible.

You are not the only one, and you don't have to go through this alone. Reach out, find support, connect with others who have been through similar pain.

There is strength in community, in knowing that others have overcome, and that you, too, can overcome.

Closing Thoughts

My journey from pain to healing has not been easy, but it has been worth it. **God has taken my brokenness and transformed it into something beautiful**—and I believe He can do the same for you. The road ahead may be long, but with God's help, you can heal, you can rebuild, and you can step into the life that God has always intended for you.

So, if you're reading this and you feel lost, hopeless, or stuck, I want you to know this: **There is hope. You are loved. You are worthy.** God has a future for you, and it's brighter than anything you can imagine.

Keep moving forward, step by step, and trust that He will make a way.

Conclusion

Moving Forward with Hope and Strength

As we close the pages of this journey, I want to leave you with a final word of encouragement: **Your past does not define you**, and the scars of your experiences do not determine your future. If there is one thing I want you to take away from these chapters, it is this: **You are not what you've been through.** You are more than the narcissistic abuse, more than the pain, more than the hurt that has tried to steal your joy and peace.

Healing is a journey—one that takes time, patience, and determination. It's not a quick fix or a single moment of breakthrough, but a process. A process that begins when you make the decision that you **will not let your pain dictate your future.** It starts with choosing to take back the power that was stolen from you. That power is **within you**, and with God's strength, you are fully capable of reclaiming your life and your joy.

As we've explored, the effects of narcissistic abuse are deep and far-reaching. The emotional scars can sometimes feel overwhelming, and it may seem like the wounds will never heal. But let me remind you—**you are stronger than you think.** Every time you choose to move forward, every time you choose to stand tall, you are reclaiming a part of yourself that was once lost. Every day you choose to **live with purpose**—to rise above your circumstances, to embrace healing, and to reject the lies of narcissism—you are becoming the person God has always intended you to be.

Throughout this book, I've shared stories and strategies to help you take back control of your life. From **owning your joy** to **finding the right support system**, the journey of healing is all about making empowered choices. But the heart of it all is knowing that you **are not alone.** No matter how isolating narcissistic abuse may feel, remember: God is with you every step of the way. You have the ultimate source of strength and comfort in Him. And you have the power to create a future that is not determined by your past.

A Life Transformed by Healing

The key to moving forward is not pretending that the past didn't happen. It's not about ignoring the pain or erasing the memories. The key is **transforming that pain into something greater**. The scars of narcissistic abuse may always be with you, but they do not have to define your story. In fact, they can become **testaments to your resilience, to your strength, to the power of God's healing in your life**.

Every scar tells a story of **victory over darkness**, of choosing to rise, of refusing to stay stuck in the prison of pain. Yes, there will be moments of doubt and despair. Yes, there will be days when the memories of abuse feel overwhelming. But each time you choose to trust God's plan, each time you choose to believe in your worth, you are rewiring your mind and soul. **You are choosing freedom.**

This freedom doesn't come from ignoring the hurt; it comes from acknowledging it and letting God use it for His glory. It comes from allowing God to take the very thing that the enemy meant for harm and turning it into something beautiful. You are living proof that **God can redeem any situation**—even the most painful, the most broken. He can restore, renew, and repurpose your life in ways that you never thought possible.

The Power of Your Story

Your story matters. The pain you've experienced, the battles you've fought, and the healing you've walked through have all shaped you into someone who is uniquely equipped to help others. By sharing your journey, you not only allow others to see the depth of God's healing power, but you also step into your calling to help those who are where you once were. You are no longer a victim of your circumstances; you are a **witness to the goodness of God**, a testimony of what's possible when you surrender your pain to Him and allow Him to lead you into freedom.

The lessons you've learned are not just for you; they are for those around you. As you continue your journey of healing, let your story be a beacon of hope for others who are struggling. Your words, your actions, your life can inspire someone who is still trapped in the darkness. **You have the power to lift others**, to show them that healing is not only possible, but that it is real and within reach.

Letting Go and Moving On
Healing also involves letting go. Letting go of the need to control every situation, letting go of the bitterness and anger that may have built up over time. It involves **forgiving**—not for the sake of the abuser, but for your own sake. Forgiveness is not about excusing the hurt; it's about freeing yourself from the chains of resentment that hold you hostage to the past.

Forgiveness is a powerful part of the healing process. When you forgive, you are not letting the abuser off the hook. You are releasing yourself from the grip of pain, resentment, and bitterness. You are choosing to **move on**, to **move forward** in peace, knowing that God's justice is perfect and that He will make all things right in His timing.

It's not easy. But it is worth it. **You are worth it.**

Hope for the Future

As you move forward, don't be afraid to dream again. Don't be afraid to believe that a future of peace, purpose, and joy is possible for you. **God has a good plan for your life**—a plan to give you a hope and a future (Jeremiah 29:11). This plan is not based on your past, but on His love and faithfulness. It's a plan that is bigger than your circumstances, greater than any pain or betrayal you've faced.

Healing is not an event; it is a journey. And with each step you take, you are getting closer to the person God designed you to be. Your healing is **already happening**, even when it doesn't feel like it. Trust in the process. Trust in God's timing. Trust that every moment of pain, every tear you've shed, will not be wasted. **God is working it all together for your good**.

So, take heart. Keep going. Keep pressing forward with hope, courage, and faith. The road ahead may not always be easy, but it will always be worth it. Your future is filled with promise, and you are stepping into it with the power of God's love behind you.

You are **healed**, you are **whole**, and your **best days are still ahead**.

Questionnaire

Are You in a Relationship with a Narcissist?

This questionnaire is designed to help you assess whether you might be in a relationship with a narcissist. Answer these questions honestly and reflect on your experiences with the person. If you answer "yes" to many of these questions, it could be an indication that the person you're dealing with exhibits narcissistic traits.

1. Grandiosity and Sense of Entitlement

- **Does this person regularly exaggerate their accomplishments, talents, or abilities?**
  (e.g., Claims they are superior or have done something that they haven't, expects to be admired without effort.)
    - ☐ Yes
    - ☐ No

- **Do they expect special treatment or believe they deserve to be treated better than others?**
  (e.g., They demand priority, want others to adjust their schedules for them, or show little appreciation for fairness.)
    - ☐ Yes
    - ☐ No

2. Lack of Empathy

- **Does this person show little or no concern for your feelings or needs?**

    (e.g., They minimize your emotions, dismiss your struggles, or make you feel like you're being overly sensitive.)

    - o ☐ Yes
    - o ☐ No

- **When you are going through something difficult, do they respond in a cold or dismissive way?**

    (e.g., They ignore your pain, are indifferent, or turn the focus back to themselves.)

    - o ☐ Yes
    - o ☐ No

3. Manipulative or Exploitative Behavior

- **Do they use others for their personal gain, without regard for how it affects them?**

    (e.g., They manipulate people to get their way, such as using guilt or charm to control others.)

    - o ☐ Yes
    - o ☐ No

- **Are you often made to feel like you're only valued when you're meeting their needs or desires?**

    (e.g., They take from you but give little in return emotionally and show little appreciation.)

    - o ☐ Yes
    - o ☐ No

4. Need for Admiration

- **Do they constantly seek praise or validation from you and others?**

    (e.g., They fish for compliments, brag about themselves, or become upset if they don't get enough admiration.)

    - ☐ Yes
    - ☐ No

- **Are they always the center of attention in social situations, and do they become upset if they're not?**

    (e.g., They often dominate conversations and steer everything back to themselves.)

    - ☐ Yes
    - ☐ No

5. Sense of Superiority

- **Do they belittle or dismiss others, especially those they perceive as less important or inferior?**

    (e.g., They are condescending or sarcastic towards people they consider "beneath" them.)

    - ☐ Yes
    - ☐ No

- **Do they act like they are always right, even when presented with evidence to the contrary?**

    (e.g., They refuse to acknowledge their mistakes and shift the blame to others.)

    - ☐ Yes
    - ☐ No

6. Emotional Reactions

- **Do they have explosive reactions or get extremely angry over small or insignificant things?**

    (e.g., They throw tantrums or become aggressive if things don't go their way.)

    - ☐ Yes
    - ☐ No

- **Do they make you feel like you're "walking on eggshells" to avoid triggering their anger or resentment?**

    (e.g., You feel nervous, anxious, or unsure about how to speak or behave around them.)

    - ☐ Yes
    - ☐ No

7. Gaslighting and Distortion of Reality

- **Do they frequently deny things they've said or done, even when you have clear evidence?**

    (e.g., They make you doubt your memory or perception of events.)

    - ☐ Yes
    - ☐ No

- **Do they make you feel like you're crazy or irrational when you question their actions or behaviors?**

    (e.g., They use phrases like "You're too sensitive" or "That didn't happen the way you remember it.")

    - ☐ Yes
    - ☐ No

8. Envy and Jealousy

- **Do they show jealousy or resentment when others succeed or receive praise?**

    (e.g., They may downplay others' achievements or criticize people who are in the spotlight.)

    - ☐ Yes
    - ☐ No

- **Do they often accuse you of being envious or jealous, even when this isn't true?**

    (e.g., They project their own feelings of jealousy onto you.)

    - ☐ Yes
    - ☐ No

9. Isolation

- **Do they try to isolate you from your family, friends, or other support networks?**

    (e.g., They criticize your loved ones or make you feel guilty for spending time with others.)

    - ☐ Yes
    - ☐ No

- **Do they get upset or angry when you want to spend time with people outside the relationship?**

    (e.g., They make you feel guilty or demand your undivided attention.)

    - ☐ Yes
    - ☐ No

10. Inconsistent or Shifting Behavior

- **Do their moods shift quickly between charm and hostility?**

  (e.g., They can be sweet and loving one moment, then cold or critical the next.)

  - ☐ Yes
  - ☐ No

- **Do they make promises or claims they don't keep or follow through on?**

  (e.g., They make grandiose promises but rarely deliver, leaving you disappointed or confused.)

  - ☐ Yes
  - ☐ No

11. Love Bombing and Idealization

- **In the early stages of the relationship, did they shower you with excessive affection, gifts, or attention?**

  (e.g., They made you feel like you were the most important person in the world, but the attention seemed to be overwhelming or too much too soon.)

  - ☐ Yes
  - ☐ No

- **Do they quickly switch from adoring you to criticizing you without warning?**

  (e.g., They may compliment you intensely one day, only to belittle you or call you names the next.)

  - ☐ Yes

- o ☐ No

12. Control and Domination

- **Do they often try to control aspects of your life, such as your schedule, friends, or career choices?**

  (e.g., They may tell you what to wear, who you should spend time with, or even what you should do for a living.)

  - o ☐ Yes
  - o ☐ No

- **Do they become angry or upset when you make decisions that don't include them or that they don't agree with?**

  (e.g., They push their opinions on you and make you feel guilty for disagreeing or making independent choices.)

  - o ☐ Yes
  - o ☐ No

13. Projection and Blame Shifting

- **Do they often accuse you of things they themselves are doing?**

  (e.g., They may accuse you of being selfish, manipulative, or dishonest when they are the ones exhibiting these behaviors.)

  - o ☐ Yes
  - o ☐ No

- **When things go wrong, do they quickly blame you or others, never taking responsibility for their actions?**

  (e.g., They rarely admit fault or make excuses, instead they point fingers at you, their environment, or circumstances.)

  - o ☐ Yes

o ☐ No

14. Inconsistent Communication and Silent Treatment

- **Do they suddenly stop communicating with you (silent treatment) when they don't get their way?**

    (e.g., They may ignore you for hours or even days, refusing to talk or address an issue, leaving you confused and uncertain.)

    o ☐ Yes

    o ☐ No

- **Do they frequently withhold affection or attention as a way to punish or control you?**

    (e.g., They withdraw emotionally, physically, or affectionately when they feel disrespected or disappointed, forcing you to "earn" their approval.)

    o ☐ Yes

    o ☐ No

15. Superficial Charm

- **Do they often appear charming or charismatic to others, but you notice a different side to them when you're alone?**

    (e.g., In public, they may be friendly, outgoing, and likable, but behind closed doors, they're cold, demanding, or dismissive.)

    o ☐ Yes

    o ☐ No

- **Do they have a history of manipulating or deceiving others to get what they want?**

    (e.g., They may have a pattern of lying or using others to serve their needs or desires.)

- o ☐ Yes
- o ☐ No

16. Competing with Others

- **Do they often feel threatened by others' success or talents, especially when it outshines their own?**

  (e.g., They may try to downplay other people's accomplishments or try to make everything a competition.)

  - o ☐ Yes
  - o ☐ No

- **Do they insist on being the best at everything, even in situations where it's not necessary or possible?**

  (e.g., They may want to dominate every conversation or event, pushing others aside to maintain their sense of superiority.)

  - o ☐ Yes
  - o ☐ No

17. Conditional Love and Approval

- **Do they make you feel like you need to "earn" their love or approval?**

  (e.g., They may tell you that you're "not good enough" or "don't deserve their affection" unless you meet their demands or expectations.)

  - o ☐ Yes
  - o ☐ No

- **Do they only show love or affection when you meet their needs but withdraw or become cold when you don't?**
  (e.g., Their affection is transactional — given only when you are fulfilling their desires.)

    - ☐ Yes

    - ☐ No

18. Chronic Victimhood and Self-Pity

- **Do they often play the victim, even when they are the one at fault?**
  (e.g., They may make you feel guilty or responsible for their unhappiness, even when they are causing the issues.)

    - ☐ Yes

    - ☐ No

- **Do they tend to exaggerate their own suffering, even in situations where they might not be as impacted as they claim?**
  (e.g., They may act as though they are always the one suffering or the one being mistreated, even when the circumstances don't support it.)

    - ☐ Yes

    - ☐ No

19. Unpredictability and Emotional Instability

- **Do they often act impulsively or unpredictably, making you feel like you're constantly walking on eggshells?**
  (e.g., Their moods can swing rapidly between extremes — from being overly affectionate to suddenly hostile or cold.)

    - ☐ Yes

    - ☐ No

- **Do they make you feel anxious or uncertain about the future of your relationship due to their unpredictability?**

    (e.g., You feel constantly anxious about whether they will accept or reject you, or if their mood will shift unexpectedly.)

    - ☐ Yes
    - ☐ No

20. Invalidation of Your Feelings

- **Do they frequently invalidate your feelings or emotions, making you question your reality?**

    (e.g., They may tell you things like, "You're overreacting," "You're too emotional," or "You're just imagining things" when you express your feelings.)

    - ☐ Yes
    - ☐ No

- **Do they dismiss your opinions or ideas as unimportant or inferior to their own?**

    (e.g., They disregard your input or ideas and try to make you feel like your perspective doesn't matter.)

    - ☐ Yes
    - ☐ No

Final Reflection:

If you answered "yes" to several of the questions, it's highly likely that you are in a relationship with a narcissistic individual. Narcissistic behavior is often emotionally and psychologically damaging, and it can be challenging to navigate. It's important to prioritize your mental and emotional well-being.

Next Steps:

- **Recognize the Signs**: Understanding the patterns of narcissism can help you protect yourself from further harm.

- **Seek Support**: Talk to trusted friends, family, or a therapist to get an outside perspective and emotional support.

- **Establish Boundaries**: Set firm boundaries to protect yourself from further manipulation or harm.

- **Consider Your Options**: If the relationship is abusive or toxic, you may need to evaluate whether it's healthy to continue the relationship.

Remember, **you are not alone** in dealing with narcissistic abuse. Healing begins with awareness and seeking the support and resources you need to reclaim your sense of self-worth and well-being.

Resource Page for Individuals Experiencing Narcissistic Abuse

Navigating the complexities of narcissistic abuse can be challenging and isolating. However, support is available, and connecting with the right resources can provide crucial assistance and guidance. The following resource pages are designed to offer a range of tools, support networks, and professional help to those who may be experiencing or recovering from narcissistic abuse.

1. Crisis Support

- **National Domestic Violence Hotline**
    - Website: [TheHotline.org] (https://www.thehotline.org)
    - Phone: 1-800-799-7233
    - Text: Text "START" to 88788
    - Description: Provides confidential support and resources for individuals experiencing domestic violence, including those who may be facing emotional abuse.

- **National Suicide Prevention Lifeline**
    - Website: [988lifeline.org] (https://988lifeline.org)
    - Phone: 988
    - Description: Offers free and confidential support 24/7 for individuals in emotional distress or crisis.

2. Therapy and Counseling

- **American Psychological Association (APA)**
    - Website: [APA.org](https://www.apa.org/helpcenter)

- o Description: Provides a directory to find licensed psychologists and therapists in your area.

- **Psychology Today Therapist Directory**
    - o Website: [PsychologyToday.com] (https://www.psychologytoday.com/us/therapists)
    - o Description: A comprehensive directory to find therapists and counselors, including those specializing in trauma and narcissistic abuse.

- **TherapyRoute.com**
    - o Website: [TherapyRoute.com] (https://www.therapyroute.com)
    - o Description: An online directory of therapists, psychologists, and counselors, searchable by location and specialty.

3. Support Groups and Communities

- **Narcissistic Abuse Recovery (Facebook Group)**
    - o Website: [Facebook.com/groups/narcissisticabuse] (https://www.facebook.com/groups/narcissisticabuse)
    - o Description: An online support group where individuals can share experiences and support each other through the recovery process.

- **Narcissistic Abuse Support Forum**
    - o Website: [NarcissisticAbuse.com] (https://www.narcissisticabuse.com)
    - o Description: Offers a forum for discussions, support, and information about recovering from narcissistic abuse.

- **Reddit: r/raisedbynarcissists**
    - o Website: [Reddit.com/r/raisedbynarcissists](https://www.reddit.com/r/raisedbynarcissists/)
    - o Description: A subreddit for individuals who grew up with narcissistic parents, providing a space for discussion and support.

- **Psych Central: Narcissistic Abuse**
    - [PsychCentral.com](https://psychcentral.com/lib/narcissistic-abuse)

- **Mental Health America**
    - [MentalHealthAmerica.net](https://www.mentalhealthamerica.net)

- **Narcissistic Abuse Recovery Program**
    - [NarcissisticAbuseRecoveryProgram.com](https://www.narcissisticabuserecoveryprogram.com)

4. Hotlines and Helplines

- **SAMHSA's National Helpline**
    - Phone: 1-800-662-HELP (4357)
    - Description: Provides confidential information and referrals for mental health and substance abuse services.

- **RAINN (Rape, Abuse & Incest National Network)**
    - Website: [RAINN.org](https://www.rainn.org)
    - Phone: 1-800-656-4673
    - Description: Offers support for survivors of sexual violence, including emotional and psychological abuse.

5. Legal Resources

- **Legal Aid Society**
    - Website: [LegalAid.org](https://www.legalaid.org)
    - Description: Provides free legal assistance and advocacy for individuals facing abuse and other legal issues.

- **National Coalition Against Domestic Violence (NCADV)**
    - Website: [NCADV.org](https://www.ncadv.org)
    - Description: Offers resources and support for individuals experiencing domestic violence, including legal resources and advocacy.

Remember: You Are Not Alone

Experiencing narcissistic abuse can be incredibly isolating, but support is available. These resources are here to offer you guidance, support, and a path to healing. Whether you are seeking immediate help, ongoing support, or educational materials, know that reaching out for help is a powerful step toward reclaiming your life and finding a place of peace and strength.

Afterword

Thank you for joining me on this journey *through From Pain to Purpose*. Crafting this guide has been a deeply personal and life-changing experience, and I am profoundly grateful for the opportunity to share my insights and experiences with you.

Your support is invaluable to me, and I sincerely hope that the strategies and reflections offered within these pages have provided you with solace and strength. My greatest hope is that you find empowerment and renewal through the principles shared in this book, and that you see the possibility for a flourishing life even after the profound challenges of narcissistic abuse.

If you have found this guide meaningful, I would be deeply appreciative if you could leave a review on Amazon and Goodreads. Your feedback is crucial, not only in supporting my journey as an author but also in helping others discover this book and its message of faith, resilience, and recovery. By sharing your thoughts, you contribute to spreading a message of hope and healing to those who may need it most.

Be sure to subscribe to my newsletter to stay informed about upcoming releases, special giveaways, and other exciting updates. Together, let's build a community dedicated to reclaiming our true selves and finding strength through our shared experiences. Thank you once again for your support and for being a part of this journey.

Cheryl Dyson-Bennett

www.cheryldysonbennett.info

You can also find me on:
Instagram
Facebook
Facebook Group

About the Author

Dr. Cheryl Dyson-Bennett is a highly esteemed life coach, acclaimed author, and sought-after motivational speaker, dedicated to guiding individuals toward realizing their highest potential. As the visionary Chief Executive Officer of Designed for Greatness, LLC, and Women of Destiny Empowerment Enterprises, Cheryl leverages her extensive experience and passion for personal development to inspire transformative growth in others.

Cheryl's literary journey began with the release of her first book *In the Arms of Jesus: Favor, Increase and Promotion*, in 2019, followed by the impactful *Divine Keys to Unlocking Your Destiny*. Since then, she has authored five additional books, each contributing to her mission of empowering and inspiring others. In addition to her books, Cheryl has created a plethora of journals designed to guide readers in their personal and spiritual growth, offering practical tools for reflection and self-discovery.

Her love for writing dates back to her childhood, when she would spend countless hours crafting stories and poems. Recognizing the profound power of her words to effect positive change, Cheryl pursued writing with a fervent dedication that has only deepened over time. Her works are infused with themes of hope, resilience, and divine guidance, drawing from her personal experiences and her unwavering belief in the power of faith and divine timing.

Cheryl's life mission is to empower women to navigate life's trials with grace and purpose, ultimately leading them to a fulfilling and purposeful existence. Her personal experiences with adversity have fortified her belief in the power of divine intervention and the importance of trusting in God's perfect timing. These challenges have not only strengthened her resolve but have also enriched her writing, making her messages of hope and transformation deeply impactful.

In addition to her roles as a life coach and author, Cheryl is a dynamic speaker who engages audiences with her heartfelt messages and practical wisdom. Her seminars and workshops have transformed the lives of many, equipping them with the tools and insights needed to overcome obstacles and seize opportunities.

Cheryl is also actively involved in various philanthropic initiatives, supporting causes related to women's empowerment and community development. Her commitment to giving back reflects her belief in the collective power of individuals to create positive change.

With an unwavering dedication to unlocking human potential, Dr. Cheryl Dyson-Bennett continues to inspire and uplift individuals, helping them navigate their journeys with confidence and purpose. Her work stands as a testament to the transformative power of faith, resilience, and the pursuit of greatness.

Cheryl Dyson-Bennett's Publications

In the Arms of Jesus: Favor, Increase, and Promotion

Divine Keys to Unlocking Your Destiny: A 30-Day Journey to Unlocking Your Destiny

Divine Keys to Letting Go: A Guide to Mastering and Unleashing the Greatness in You, Let Go, and Take Charge of Your Life

Jesus Loves Me

Illuminating Your Path with God's Word: A 52-Guided Devotional to Enlighten Your Journey through Daily Prayers and Confessions

Till Betrayal Do Us Part: A Memoir of Surviving Narcissistic Abuse

Moving Past the Hurt: Reclaiming Your Identity in Christ

Journals

Pray, Trust, Wait, and Repeat

Divine Keys to Letting Go Prayer Journal

Anointed and Appointed Prayer Journal

I Am Blessed and Highly Favored Journal

Phenomenal Woman Prayer Journal

Get ready for Cheryl's highly anticipated upcoming book, *Moving Past the Hurt: Reclaiming Your Identity in Christ*. In this transformative work, Cheryl dives deep into the journey of healing from past wounds, offering spiritual insights and practical tools to help you rediscover your God-given identity. With her signature blend of heartfelt encouragement and faith-based wisdom, this book promises to be a powerful resource for anyone seeking to overcome pain, rebuild self-worth, and embrace a future filled with purpose and hope. Stay tuned for its release—you won't want to miss this life-changing guide to reclaiming your identity in Christ!

www.ingramcontent.com/pod-product-compliance
Lightning Source LLC
Chambersburg PA
CBHW070505100426
42743CB00010B/1760